Kenkey Economics

Principles of Sustainable Wealth Creation

Franklin Adatsi

ISBN:1516924525
ISBN-13:9781516924523

To my lovely daughter, Maria Adatsi-Fernandez, whose birth inspired me to write this book in an effort to encourage broader economic and financial literacy, especially among young people.

CONTENTS

Acknowledgments

ACKNOWLEDGMENTS

I would like to thank God for giving me the inspiration to write this book. Inspiration is critical to conceiving and completing any meaningful work of art.

My parents have been highly influential in my life. They have always encouraged me to explore and learn. I am grateful for their patience and confidence.

The world is full of teachers but there are few great coaches. I am indebted to Wendy De-Youngster, Charlotte Acheampong and Ignacio Palacios-Huerta, for their dedication to "coaching learners" rather than "instructing students" and their ability to inspire intellectual curiosity among their students.

My employers and work colleagues have helped me to develop a better understanding of financial markets and to appreciate the principles of value creation in businesses. I am privileged to have been mentored by Peter Hollis, Ronnie Petrie and Ross Teverson.

In the process of writing this book, I had many fruitful discussions with Paa Kwesi Imbeah who provided great insights. The quality of this book would not be the same without his ideas and would have only been better if I had the opportunity to spend more time with him. I am indebted to Paa for his great contribution and for maintaining an open house policy at all times.

Special thanks to my dear wife, Elena, for supporting me through the process, providing insightful feedback, and helping out with a disproportionate share of childcare. I admire your passion for education.

1

THE ECONOMY AND WHY IT MATTERS

The annual labour of every nation is the fund which originally supplies it with all the necessaries and conveniences of life which it annually consumes.
—Adam Smith, father of modern economics (1723–1790)

The economy of a country refers to the large variety of productive activities that create value for people. The size of the economy is determined by the *value* of goods and services produced by all workers in a country over a given period. Focusing on *value* captures the quantity of production as well as the quality. The economy grows when workers increase the production of desirable goods and services.

The total value of production in a given year translates into income (wages) for employees, income and profits for business owners, and tax revenue for governments. The annual economic output is the source of income that pays for *consumption* of goods and services, *investment*, *government spending* on public services, and the consumption of desirable goods produced in other countries (over and above what a country sells abroad). The value of the annual production determines the scope and quality of products and services that residents in a country can access and afford.

Economic growth supports the greater availability and affordability of desirable products, which help to improve living standards. Economic growth occurs when a country's citizens (or residents) and businesses are growing the value of goods and services they produce. Economic growth translates into better job opportunities, higher wages, increased profits, greater investment opportunities, and an increase in government tax revenue (a beneficiary of rising profits and wages). By contrast, economic contraction reflects a decline in the value of production as well as average income levels. When the economy contracts, the financial prospects for employees and firms become poorer, unemployment rises as businesses cut back on production and investment, government revenue shrinks as the tax base decreases (the number of taxpayers decreases, and their income falls), and the provision of public services may suffer as a result.

The responsibility for improving living standards lies with everyone living in a society. Policies and business practices that reward value creation can stimulate the development of activities that support economic growth. A large number of innovations have created tremendous value for people by making it more convenient and cheaper to access desirable products and services. For example, innovations and improvements in air and sea travel as well as the development of the Internet have lowered the cost of transportation and communication around world. Faster and cheaper travel and communication opportunities make it more convenient for people to interact with each other. Lower transportation cost increases the gains from trade. Desirable goods produced in other regions of the world that were once beyond the reach of most people partly because of high transportation costs, have now become more accessible at affordable prices. Innovation in transportation has therefore created immense value for society and supported higher living standards.

The Gross Domestic Product (GDP) is the most widely used measure of economic output over a given period. Comparing the value of economic output (GDP) over time helps to quantitatively assess the extent to which a country or region is producing more (economic growth) or less value (economic contraction). A key component of policy initiatives of every government targets the creation of favorable conditions to stimulate economic growth in order to improve living standards.

The standard of living in a country depends on the productivity of its workers. People are interested in improving their levels of affordability for desirable goods and services. Affordability levels improve with employee productivity. Productivity measures the value of goods and services that a typical worker is capable of producing over a given period. In countries where workers are able to produce significantly more (as a result of technology investments and good business practices), the higher level of production is typically accompanied by lower prices of goods in relation to average wages. Greater availability of products at lower prices, increases the level of affordability for the general public. Rising productivity means that, the same amount of inputs or resources are utilized to produce a greater quantity of desirable goods. As workers and businesses create more value out of the resources they employ, the unit cost of production falls, which increases affordability and living standards for the population.

Over the past decades, many consumer products have become more affordable, i.e., the cost of consumer goods has fallen relative to income levels, because of productivity improvements in manufacturing. For example, if it takes a shoemaker a whole day to produce one pair of shoes, the price he will charge for the pair has to be sufficient to pay for the cost of materials as well as his cost of living for a day. However, if technology allows the average shoemaker to produce ten pairs of shoes per day, the higher level of productivity is likely to translate into a lower cost of shoes for everyone. The shoemaker's daily wage is now spread over ten pairs of shoes, and each pair will cost less as a result.

The productivity of workers in a country determines income levels and living standards. Higher productivity translates into greater affordability (i.e. lower prices relative to average wages) and rising living standards.

High living standards occur when employee or household wages command high levels of affordability. It is the purchasing power of wages rather than the absolute amount of income earned that determines living standards. The purchasing power measures the amount of goods and services that a given amount of money can buy. The purchasing power of wages or household income is determined by productivity levels in the economy. People living in "rich" or "high-income" countries enjoy high levels of affordability, because workers in these countries produce much more. The typical worker in a "high-income" country produces more cars, TVs, computers, agricultural produce—a greater quantity of highly valued products and services than the average worker in a "poor" or "low-income" country. In a "high-income" country, the large amount of production lowers the price of goods when compared to typical household or employee wages. In other words, typical employee or household wages command higher levels of affordability in more productive countries. Policies that encourage individuals and businesses to undertake investments that improve productivity (producing more, relative to the amount of resources employed) have the potential to improve living standards. As productivity increases, more efficient use of resources lowers the cost of production and the price of goods, when compared to household income levels.

High productivity economies are often referred to as "high-income" countries because average employee wages command high levels of affordability. At high levels of productivity, many more goods are produced in relation to the amount of resources employed. As a result, the cost of basic goods and services is low when compared to average employee wages (i.e., high levels of affordability). Countries with low levels of productivity are often referred to as "low income" countries because at low levels of productivity the cost of basic goods and services is high when compared to average wages (i.e., low levels of affordability).

The productivity level in a country can be evaluated by measuring the value of economic output per person or GDP per capita. In assessing living standards in countries, it is important to adjust the value of economic output (GDP) for the population size in order to measure the productivity of the population. A country with a very large population is likely to have a large economic output, because there are many more workers contributing to its total production. However, productivity levels or the value of production per person—which is most important in determining living standards—may not necessarily be high.

For example, figure 1.1 shows that India has a very large economic output ($1.8 trillion in 2013, the tenth-largest economy in the world). Its large output is produced by a very large population of over one billion people. As a result, the productivity or value of economic production per person in India is less impressive. Low productivity in India translates into lower levels of affordability when compared to countries like Korea and Mexico, that generate a lower economic output in absolute terms, but a much higher value of output per person (greater productivity).

The value of economic output per person (GDP per capita) provides useful information about affordability levels and living standards across countries. Comparing productivity levels across countries involves using a common currency such as the US dollar as a base. Using the dollar to facilitate comparisons is simple and straightforward, but it may understate the purchasing power or living standards in low-income countries where a lower cost of labour translates into a lower cost of producing basic goods and services. A dollar of income commands a higher purchasing power in a low-income country than in a high-income country. The GDP per person measured at Purchasing Power Parity (PPP) attempts to create a more accurate measure of productivity and living standards, particularly in poor countries, by taking account of the differences in the cost of producing comparable goods in various countries.

An economy can grow through an increase in its population (or number of workers). However, for income levels or living standards to rise, the rate of economic growth has to be higher than the growth rate of the population. In other words, the average person or worker has to produce more in order to earn a higher income. Living standards cannot meaningfully improve over time without sustainable gains in productivity.

Figure 1.1   Income and Productivity Levels around the World (2013 figures)

Countries Ranked by GDP per Person	Value of Economic Output (GDP, US$ billion)	Population Size (millions of people)	GDP per person in $ based on exchange rates	GDP per person in $ based on purchasing power parity	Life Expectancy (years)
United States	16,800	316	53,101	53,101	80
Germany	3,636	81	44,999	40,007	81
France	2,737	66	41,475	35,784	82
United Kingdom	2,536	64	39,567	37,307	81
Japan	4,901	127	38,591	36,300	83
Korea	1,222	50	24,329	33,189	81
Russia	2,118	143	14,819	17,884	70
Venezuela	374	30	12,472	13,605	74
Brazil	2,243	200	11,311	12,221	76
Turkey	827	75	10,815	15,353	74
Mexico	1,259	122	10,630	15,563	76
Colombia	382	48	8,098	11,189	75
China	9,181	1,367	6,747	9,844	76
Peru	207	30	6,674	11,124	75
Algeria	206	39	5,438	7,534	73
Indonesia	870	250	3,510	5,214	72
Egypt	271	82	3,226	6,579	73
Philippines	272	98	2,790	4,682	66
Ghana	44	26	1,730	3,461	66
Nigeria	286	173	1,692	2,831	53
India	1,871	1,252	1,505	4,077	64
Pakistan	237	182	1,302	4,600	66
Cameroon	28	22	1,271	2,423	62
Zimbabwe	13	14	987	788	54
Ethiopia	48	94	542	1,366	61
D.R. Congo	31	68	451	648	49

Sources: World Bank; IMF; Author

Some economic activities have the potential to create far greater value than others. For two countries that are comparable in terms of population size and employment opportunities, differences in productivity and living standards will be determined primarily by the quantity of goods produced in each country. If the majority of workers in two countries of comparable population size are primarily employed in steel production, the country that produces more steel will command a higher income level. If one of these countries were to develop the technology to competitively produce goods that have a higher value, such as cars, citizens of that country will be more likely to enjoy a significant rise in income levels or living standards. The value of cars produced could be multiple times the value of the annual production of steel. The key components in a car are made of steel and other basic materials. The price of steel is about $500 a ton and yet at car which weighs 1.5 tons may cost up to $30,000 dollars. The significant difference between the price of a car and that of steel can be attributed to the technology and skills employed by workers and businesses that use steel as a raw material to create the high value-added components in a car. Because of their higher level of productivity, people living in countries where workers are primarily employed in the production of highly valued goods and services will tend to command higher income levels than residents of countries where the majority of workers is focused on producing low-valued items (e.g., agricultural commodities, steel and other basic materials etc.).

The value of output (per person) much more than the quantity of output is most relevant in determining income levels and living standards. Residents of countries that produce more high value-added products command higher income levels and living standards.

Figure 1.2. There is a Strong Relationship between Productivity and Living standards

Sources: World Bank; International Monetary Fund.

Over the past two centuries, rising global productivity, on the back of advances in technology and greater international cooperation, has resulted in great gains in living standards in all countries. Compared to wealthy families in previous generations, the poor in many countries today, have superior access to healthcare, education, nutrition, transportation and other services. Living standards have improved in all countries over this period. Today, the life expectancy in some of the poorest nations in the world is significantly higher than that of the most technologically advanced nations at the beginning of the twentieth century. Through greater international cooperation, the benefits of technological advancement and productivity gains have spread throughout the world and supported higher living standards.

Figure 1.3.

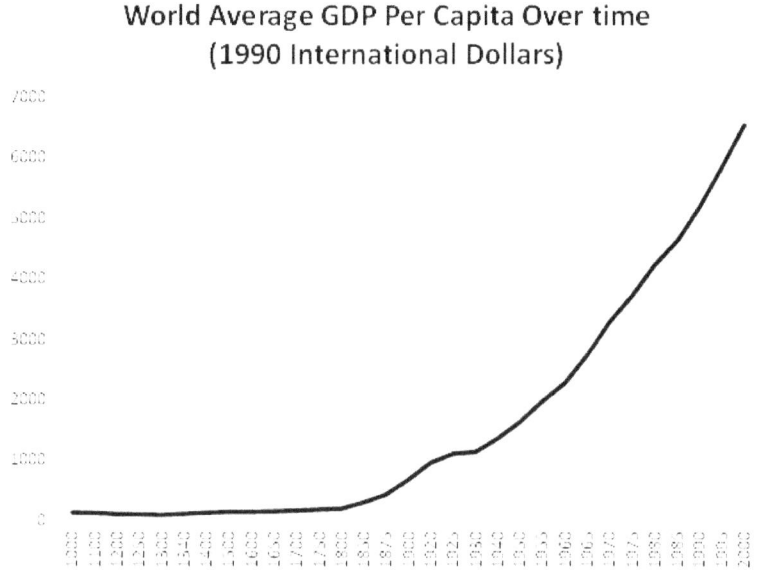

Source: DeLong, J. Brad. 1998. "Estimates of World GDP, One Million BC to Present."

Income levels and living standards are dependent on the current levels of productivity in an economy. A considerable number of productive initiatives support the existing level of production and living standards in an economy. Sustaining current levels of production (i.e., no economic growth), requires the same level of effort, resources and techniques to be applied year after year. When productive initiatives decline, the economy is likely to contract, and living standards will fall. While economic growth is desirable, it is important to realize that the effort and attention required to sustain a given level of production cannot be taken for granted. Sustaining current levels of production is preferable to undergoing economic contraction. In order to raise living standards, the productivity of workers has to improve over time.

Case Study 1.1.

The Shipwreck Economy: Linking Economic Growth to Rising Living Standards

The single product economy. A group of shipwrecked travelers were stranded on an island thousands of miles away from their home. Within weeks they ran out of food. Pressed by their desire to survive, they decided to farm potatoes, the only source of raw food that survived the wreck. At this stage, the value of economic output is equal to the quantity of potatoes that the shipwreck survivors are able to produce, and their quality of life will be determined by the quantity of potatoes produced by each worker. Because the only product on the island is potatoes, the quality of life can be improved through techniques that allow each worker to produce more potatoes. For the most part, the availability of food (potatoes) was no longer a major concern, but there were occasionally periods of food shortages and starvation. Because the islanders depended solely on potatoes for their survival, a poor harvest due to crop diseases or lack of rain severely affected food supply. The dependence on one economic activity for income meant that the islanders' living standards were more prone to drastic changes.

Rising productivity and innovation drive economic growth and higher living standards. One day, an islander discovered how to make fishing nets out of dried potato leaves. Some islanders took up fishing and traded excess fish for potatoes. For the first time, diets on the island improved considerably with the addition of fish, and the islanders celebrated this improvement with a large festival. Supported by further innovation in farming and fishing techniques, the quantities of both potatoes and fish increased, creating more value and improving the quality of life (people were better fed).

After much experimentation, an islander discovered a special recipe for a dish of potatoes and fish seasoned with selected island spices. This generated a lot of demand from neighbours and other islanders. In response to higher than expected demand, the islander who discovered the recipe, decided to quit farming and fishing and open a restaurant. Adding a desirable dish to available consumption opportunities was a further boost to the quality of life on the island.

Higher income levels support the provision of public services and promote foreign trade. One day, while prospecting a different region of the island, an islander discovered gold. The gold discovery provided islanders with a new economic activity—one that generated higher income. With this new wealth, the islanders decided to set up a professional government of paid, full-time workers to regulate the gold-mining industry and provide public services, such as schools and hospitals on the island. Each islander agreed to contribute a proportion of his or her produce (in potatoes, restaurant meals, fish, or gold) to pay for government services. As more gold was discovered, islanders devoted more time to mining gold and less to potato farming. The value of their gold production was so high that they could afford to satisfy their entire year's requirement of potatoes by buying from a neighboring island with less than a month's wages from the gold mine. Higher income levels enabled islanders to afford other desirable products, such as medicine and mining equipment, that were not produced on the island and had to be imported from elsewhere.

Rising economic growth supports proliferation of value-added services. As the value of production on the island increased, income (affordability) levels also increased. Growing wealth in a society, makes it worthwhile for talented individuals and groups to devote their resources into creating value-added services such as entertainment, banking, medical services, and higher education. Access to a greater variety of desirable services further improves living standards. The income earned from all the economic activities on the island is spent on consumption (food, entertainment, and services), government spending (roads, schools, hospitals, etc.), investment (by households and businesses) and paying for desirable goods produced in other countries (medicines and mining equipment). As the value of production increased, the affordability of a more diverse range of desirable goods and services was enhanced, and the welfare of islanders improved immensely compared to earlier periods.

******

Diversification of economic activities supports greater stability in living standards. As seen in the shipwreck economy, the concentration of economic activity and employment in one main industry (in this case, potato production) can create sharp swings in income levels and living standards when the prospects of that industry changes. When the shipwreck economy only produced potatoes, one poor harvest due to unfavourable weather conditions could be catastrophic. Economic diversification reduces the risk of sharp swings in income levels and living standards. With a more diversified range of economic activities, negative developments in one industry are likely to be offset by growth in other industries, and even in the absence of growth in other industries, diversification reduces the direct economic impact (on employment opportunities and income) of any one industry and therefore supports more stable economic development.

The economy can grow as well as contract. The decline of any value-creating activity, if not offset by the growth of other economic activities, will lower income levels in a country. In the case of the shipwrecked island, gold is an important contributor to the overall value of production. If the price of gold collapsed, its value contribution to the economy would be much lower even if the quantity of gold produced remained unchanged. A collapse in the gold price would reduce miners' income and lower employment opportunities in mining. The declining value of production would also reduce government tax revenue, which might result in cuts to public services and government employee salaries. Overall, the reduction in the value of economic output from declining gold prices would depress employment opportunities, income levels, and reduce the standard of living on the island. In countries that generate a meaningful proportion of economic value from natural resources, sharp changes in commodity prices, over which citizens have little control, can result in large swings in income levels and living standards.

Economic growth is not a perfect measure of all activities that improve living standards. Productivity levels (GDP per person) is highly relevant in determining living standards, but it is not a perfect measure of the well-being of residents in a country. As a quantitative measure, GDP cannot account for the value of activities that positively or negatively affect our living standards in cases where there is no market (and therefore no price) for such activities or where these activities are intangible and cannot be measured. For example, GDP does not reflect the value of desirable assets and activities such as personal relationships, parental love, home cooking, community volunteering, and religious services. Furthermore, the value of economic output (GDP) may fully reflect the value of a desirable item produced in a country without taking into account any negative side effects associated with the production or use of such items. For example, even though people derive immense benefits from using electricity and driving cars, the desirability of these services may be somewhat reduced by the pollution they cause. However, this negative side effect of an otherwise desirable product is not reflected in the measured value of economic output (GDP). In other words, in some cases, the GDP may overstate the value that citizens derive from these useful products.

The power of regulation to improve living standards may increase with high levels of productivity. Because GDP per capita (or the level of productivity) is not a perfect measure of living standards, policy makers try to make up for the shortfall with regulation. Regulation that aims to reduce the effect of pollution or cap working hours, so that people can spend more time with their families, tends to put negative pressure on economic growth by increasing the cost of doing business. For example, a power generation company may have to spend more money to install pollution reduction technologies or pay penalties for excess pollution, which may increase the cost of electricity for most people. Countries that have developed high levels of productivity (i.e., "high-income" countries), have greater ability to absorb or adapt to these regulatory driven costs without a material reduction in living standards. Such countries are more likely to have effective laws that protect the rights of workers, protect the environment, and support other regulatory initiatives that improve living standards.

Economic growth and income inequality. Economic growth provides a big-picture view of the overall level of productivity increases and income growth in an economy but does not analyze how a nation's income is distributed among the population. Changes in economic output affect everyone, but some segments of the population may be affected more than others. In some cases, there might be a danger, or a perception that policies that promote economic growth may generate wealth for a fraction of the population without benefiting the average citizen. Income inequality is often associated with poverty, but there is a major distinction. Poverty refers to the inability of large segments of a population to afford basic goods and services such as food, shelter, education and healthcare. It is possible to have high levels of income inequality but low levels of poverty in a country. At extreme levels, both poverty and income inequality are undesirable. Government policy can be instrumental in addressing poverty and income-inequality problems. The provision of social services such as education and healthcare, income support measures such as regulating for adequate minimum wage levels and a tax system that demands a greater contribution from higher income households can help reduce poverty and income inequality.

Economic growth supports employment creation and poverty reduction. Economic growth stimulates the development of new economic activities and supports the expansion of existing ones. Investment creates greater employment and wage growth opportunities. Rising productivity enables more goods to be produced at lower prices (relative to wage levels). Through rising employment opportunities and greater purchasing power of wages, economic growth has the potential to lift households out of poverty.

There is strong evidence to suggest that economic growth immensely improves living conditions for the poor. Over the past two decades, strong global economic growth and the benefits of globalization have promoted the fastest reduction in poverty levels in human history. The World Bank estimates that between 1980 and 2010, the number of people living in extreme poverty (on less than $1.25 a day) around the world, fell by almost one billion people. Most of that reduction occurred between 2000 and 2010, a period of strong global economic growth, particularly in countries like China, India, and Brazil, that enjoyed the greatest reduction in extreme poverty levels. There are now less than a billion people living in extreme poverty, and the percentage of the world's population living in extreme poverty has fallen from over 50 percent in the early eighties to under 20 percent in recent years.

The economy is constantly changing under the influence of new opportunities and challenges. Proactively embracing this inevitable dynamism can support greater productivity and higher living standards in the long-term. Sustainable economic growth is derived from a dynamic process that involves the reallocation of resources to more productive activities from activities that create less value. For example, in the shipwreck economy, the discovery of gold meant that more human resources (labour) were allocated from potato farming (a low value activity) to mining gold (a higher value activity). As providers of labour (a key resource for production), workers look for more rewarding opportunities to apply their skills and will typically leave low wage jobs for higher income jobs. Capital, management time, and employees are key resources of businesses. Business owners and managers are continually looking for better avenues to employ resources in order to generate greater economic value.

The dynamism of the economy stems from daily decisions made in households, businesses, and governments with the common goal of improving their economic prospects. Innovation in technology and processes that improve the productivity of labour and lower the cost of production can stimulate economic growth. This constant evolution generates significant value and employment in new, vibrant industries but may also render some other industries (and associated jobs) redundant. The inevitable danger of suffering job losses in declining industries, as part of the process of reallocating resources to create greater economic value for society, can be a major concern for governments, businesses, and households. Governments and businesses that are more proactive in embracing this inevitable change with dynamic institutions and a productivity oriented and flexible labour mind-set are more likely to generate the greatest gains from new opportunities while also reducing the economic and social cost associated with declining industries.

All economic growth is not created equal. Quality of growth matters. Economic growth, no matter the source, is always better than no growth or economic contraction. However, the quality of growth is equally important and helps to determine the sustainability of income levels and living standards. Economic growth paints a big-picture view of how income levels may be improving. It is important to drill down to identify the key drivers of growth in order to assess the sustainability. For example, an economy that grows rapidly on the back of rising commodity prices may be less likely to sustain high income levels, because the growth driver (i.e., the commodity price) can be highly unpredictable. On the other hand, an economy that grows at a more measured pace, primarily as a result of improved business practices and the adoption of better technology across a wide range of industries, is more likely to sustain higher income and employment levels, because the growth drivers may be more sustainable and are less dependent on one industry.

A knowledge economy is essential to sustain productivity gains and improvement in living standards over the long term. The natural properties of physical resources such as land, real estate, hard labour, and metals have limitations. For example, about two tons of iron ore are needed (in combination with coke and limestone) to produce one ton of steel. It is possible to introduce efficiencies to improve the conversion rate, but the potential for improvement may be limited without substantial breakthroughs in technology.

The potential for human creativity and imagination has considerably fewer limitations. In a knowledge based economy, innovations in technology and business practices offer far greater opportunities to deliver sustainable productivity gains. For example, while productivity gains in steelmaking may be limited, advances in technology may help to develop lower cost materials that have more desirable properties. Human creativity and imagination have the capacity to put together natural resources in an infinite number of combinations to create value. The productivity gains derived from a knowledge economy ("software") may therefore be more sustainable than those derived primarily from extracting natural resources ("hardware").

A knowledge economy has the potential to improve productivity across all industries (including natural resource extraction industries). Technological innovation in one industry often has spillover effects that help to improve productivity in several other industries. Consequently, in a knowledge economy, an industry that is far removed from the epicenter of technological innovation may develop much higher levels of productivity compared to a comparable industry in a low knowledge economy. Countries where education systems encourage creativity, critical thinking, and research initiatives, and where financial markets embrace entrepreneurial initiatives are more likely to generate sustainable gains in productivity and living standards.

2

DRIVERS OF ECONOMIC GROWTH

PRICE DISCOVERY PROMOTES EFFICIENT ALLOCATION OF RESOURCES

The price setting process. Economic resources are limited in supply, and desirable products and services are costly to deliver. Prices are set to reflect the cost of resources employed in the production of goods. The cost of the labour (wages) employed to transform raw materials into finished products or to deliver a service forms a major component of the cost of production and the price of goods. Products that can only be produced by relying on a considerable number of workers typically have a high price. Products that rely on highly skilled and therefore more expensive labour (e.g. engineers employed in aircraft design and production) may also have a high price. The large influence of the cost of labour on product prices is key to understanding how productivity of workers influences affordability levels and living standards across countries. When workers are more productive, the cost of labour is spread over a larger quantity of products. This brings down the unit cost of production and makes products more affordable. In addition to raw materials and labour, capital is an essential element in the production of goods and services. The capital employed in a business typically consists of funds invested in factories and equipment and funds used in purchasing supplies. In a competitive market, the sustainable price of a good is the price that is required to pay a "fair" compensation for all the resources employed (labour, raw materials, and capital) in the production of that good.

When prices of goods rise above the cost of production, producers make more profit. Suppliers respond to rising profits by employing more workers and capital to increase production. When prices fall, supplier profits suffer. Producers respond by cutting the amount of production and reducing labour and capital resources employed in production. Some suppliers may be more efficient (i.e., have the ability to produce at a lower cost) than others such that when prices fall, in addition to suppliers reducing production, the least efficient may also go out of business.

Consumers of products and services, on the other hand, are likely to increase the quantity of goods they buy when prices fall and reduce the quantity they purchase when prices rise. Falling prices increase affordability, while rising prices make goods less

19

affordable for buyers. Consumers display varying levels of affordability and desirability for products. When prices rise, all consumers are worse off. The quantity demanded by consumers falls because, at the higher price, only those with high levels of income and those who derive the most value from a product are likely to purchase it.

Prices adjust to bring supply and demand into balance. The interaction between the ability of consumers to buy a product (demand) and the cost at which suppliers are able to produce (supply) determines the price of a product. This interaction is a dynamic process because consumers' affordability and appetite, and suppliers' input costs change over time. Through the interaction of buyers and sellers (demand and supply), prices adjust until the quantity of goods produced is matched by the quantity that consumers are willing and able to buy. The price at which consumer demand matches the quantity of production is *the market-clearing price or the equilibrium price*. At the market clearing price, there is no material surplus (excess production) or shortage (excess demand). Producers are able to sell all that they produce, and consumers are able to buy all that they can afford, at that price.

When there is a major reduction in the supply of an item (due to low levels of production), prices rise to reflect the limited supply, and only those consumers who are willing to pay the higher price will obtain the product. At the much higher price, the lower quantity of goods demanded by consumers matches the limited supply. When prices rise, producers are encouraged to invest to increase production. As the quantity of production increases, prices fall in order to attract the larger number of buyers needed to match the higher level of available supply. When advances in technology increase the amount of goods that can be produced relative to the resources employed (rising productivity), supply increases and, at the same time, prices fall to entice more people to buy. Goods that are limited in supply or costly to produce (e.g., city center apartments are limited in supply, and aircraft is expensive to produce) tend to have high prices, while goods that are widely available and less costly to produce (e.g., agricultural commodities, water, and paper) have low prices.

When buyers and sellers interact freely, prices adjust toward an equilibrium price or market clearing price. At the market clearing price, producers are able to sell their total production, and consumers who are willing to pay the market price can buy as much as they want, the market clears, and there is no surplus or shortage. When the price setting process is interrupted (e.g., by government regulation), prices can move away from the market clearing price, and shortages or surpluses become more likely.

Shortages or surpluses arise when prices deviate from the market clearing price. A surplus (excess supply or less than adequate demand) arises when producers set prices that are higher than the affordability levels of consumers. For example, high vacancy rates for apartments are likely to occur when rent levels are set above the market clearing price. When rent levels adjust lower, there is greater interest in renting, and occupancy rates improve. A shortage (excess demand or less than adequate supply) arises when prices are set below the market clearing price. For example, when a government imposes rent controls that caps rent levels below the market clearing price, the artificially low levels of rent create strong demand among consumers and limit the supply of rental property. The net effect is that a large number of people who are willing to rent at the regulated price may not be able to access rental property. In the absence of rent controls, if there is a fundamental increase in the demand for housing (e.g., because of strong economic growth and job creation in a city), property prices and rents will adjust upward. Rising property prices make it more attractive for capital providers to invest in building new rental properties to increase supply.

Mechanisms that promote price discovery enable more efficient allocation of resources and support economic growth. The development of markets (several buyers and sellers) for products allows for price discovery. Price discovery offers useful information that enables individuals, businesses, and governments to make informed economic choices to improve their well-being. Through this process, price discovery can enable a more efficient allocation of resources and support higher living standards. Prices help us to form an objective basis for assessing the value we derive from a given product. Every consumer or producer faces a large number of possible consumption or production choices. A typical supermarket may have thousands of lines of items for sale. How do people cope with choosing among the thousands of options available? Prices are the essential element that help people to determine the optimal basket of items to consume or produce.

Prices are instrumental in helping people make economic decisions. Prices are the special elements that make it possible for individuals and businesses to optimally allocate their resources among the large number of possible consumption and investment opportunities available in any country.

The decision to consume a product or a service is only made when the value it generates for the consumer is greater than (or at least equal to) the price the consumer pays. By comparing prices across a large range of products to the value derived from each product, consumers are better able to make informed decisions to optimize the benefits they derive from their income. Prices of products as well as price changes provide information about economic incentives. As price levels change in the economy, people react to this new information by changing their consumption choices. Price information helps producers to decide the type of goods to produce as well as the quantity to produce. Suppliers produce more when prices and profits rise and less when prices fall. When markets are non-existent or less developed, there is no reliable price information. Without reliable price information, decision making becomes complicated and less optimal.

Financial markets provide price information that enable firms with the most promising prospects to attract more capital resources for expansion (at the expense of less efficient firms). By supporting the efforts of firms that create the most value for society, financial markets promote economic growth and higher living standards. In periods when profit growth and investment opportunities are improving for a broad spectrum of firms, financial markets provide reliable information about the potential for higher returns on capital in the form of rising stock prices and interest rates. This price information helps stimulate a greater amount of savings to satisfy the higher capital needs in the economy. When firms have less attractive prospects, the potential return on capital falls. Financial markets enable a timely transmission of this information in the form of lower interest rates and falling stock prices to providers of capital (savers). When the expected return on capital is low, capital providers may maximize their welfare by investing less and consuming more.

In labour markets, when information about job opportunities and wage levels are more transparent, firms and employees are more successful in matching employee skills to job requirements. Reliable information about wage levels and working conditions is instrumental in helping people make decisions on how to allocate their time and financial resources for higher education and skills training. High wage levels in certain jobs may encourage a larger number of people to devote considerable time and effort into training for those jobs. For example, whereas graduates from leading universities in a number of developing countries primarily target job opportunities in the public sector and state controlled firms, graduates from top universities in the United States are mostly attracted to jobs in finance and technology. The allocation decision may be driven by higher wage levels of finance industry jobs (relative to other employment opportunities) in the United States and higher wage levels of public sector jobs in developing countries. When the relative wage levels of jobs change over time, people respond to these changes by adjusting their skills training initiatives. Greater access to labour market information can support higher levels of employment and potentially higher levels of job satisfaction.

The availability of reliable market prices for products helps both consumers and producers to make more informed decisions about how to allocate their capital for consumption and investment. When prices are distorted by government regulation, it impedes the ability of consumers and producers to optimize the allocation of resources. For example, when the government imposes limits (caps) on fuel and other utility prices, this may cause shortages when regulated prices are set below the true market price (i.e., the price that matches supply with demand). The artificially low price creates a much larger demand among consumers than what suppliers are able to produce at that price. When regulated prices are lower than true market prices, a large number of willing buyers (at the regulated price) become frustrated because they are not able to access the product. There may be other costs associated with regulatory interventions in the market. For example, the false signal about the true cost of fuel may result in excess demand and long queues when there is a shortage. It may also stimulate the growth of an illegal market that provides a reliable source of fuel at higher prices. In the absence of reliable fuel supply, many firms may be forced to curtail their operations and this may reduce employment opportunities in the economy.

Prices are essential tools for decision making. When regulators interfere in the price-setting process, they may send the wrong signals about the true economic cost of goods and services and spawn inefficient resource allocation decisions. For example, countries that heavily subsidize energy costs tend to consume much more energy than comparable countries that pay the true economic price for energy. Subsidizing energy costs reduces the incentive to invest in energy efficient cars, lighting, and other equipment. When the labour market is distorted by a large influential player, such as the government who sets wages on welfare grounds, the connection between employee productivity and wages may become weaker, and employees are less likely to invest in skills training to improve their productivity. Lower levels of productivity may ultimately contribute to an erosion in living standards. The manner in which people utilize "free" or subsidized public services such as healthcare and education (for which there is poor price information) would likely change if they had granular price information about how much it cost the government (or taxpayers) to provide these services. The availability of price information for public services may have an effect on the way people utilize these services (even when there is no direct out-of-pocket cost to the user).

Technology and mechanisms that reduce the cost of accessing and processing information can stimulate productivity gains and economic growth. In the nineteenth and twentieth centuries, the telegraph, radio, print media, and the fixed-line telephone were instrumental in transmitting information around the world. In the twenty-first century, the Internet and advances in computer technology have reduced the cost of accessing and processing information and enabled people to make faster and more informed economic decisions. This frees up time and financial resources that can be deployed into greater economic or social activities to support higher living standards. Even in situations where markets were previously well developed, the Internet has accelerated the transmission mechanism of information and encouraged greater use of price information for allocation decisions. For example, in financial markets, the Internet has made it feasible for a larger number of people to access information about investment opportunities and allocate their capital in a cheaper, faster and more convenient way. The internet has stimulated greater efficiency (lower costs and therefore lower prices for consumers) in the airline and retail industries by enabling greater price discovery among consumers.

Innovation in engineering, computer technology, medicine, agriculture, and business practices have stimulated economic growth and supported rising living standards. Innovation generates new ideas that have the potential to improve how we live and work. The creation of new desirable products and processes enable us to better tackle historic challenges and improve our standards of living. The ability of innovation to improve human life has been experienced in every corner of the world. Innovation in one industry often has a ripple effect through the economy by supporting the development of new industries and creating new jobs. Below are a few examples of transformational innovations over the past century.

The introduction of water treatment techniques and the widespread adoption of childhood vaccination have supported transformational gains in life expectancy. The introduction of water filtration and chlorination in public water supply, starting in the early part of the twentieth century, supported a drastic reduction in bacterial infections and mortality rates. Water treatment and the widespread adoption of vaccination may have contributed to the greatest gains ever in mortality reduction and improvement in life expectancy. Between 1900 and 1960, death from infectious diseases in the United States fell by almost 90 percent and life expectancy rose from fifty to seventy years. These immense and unprecedented gains have been experienced all over the world. A number of diseases such as smallpox and polio have been entirely eradicated through global vaccination programs. The growing penetration of clean water supplies and vaccination programs, in a number of developing countries, continues to support gains in life expectancy and living standards.

Figure 2.1. US Death Rate from Infectious Diseases (per 100,000 people per year)

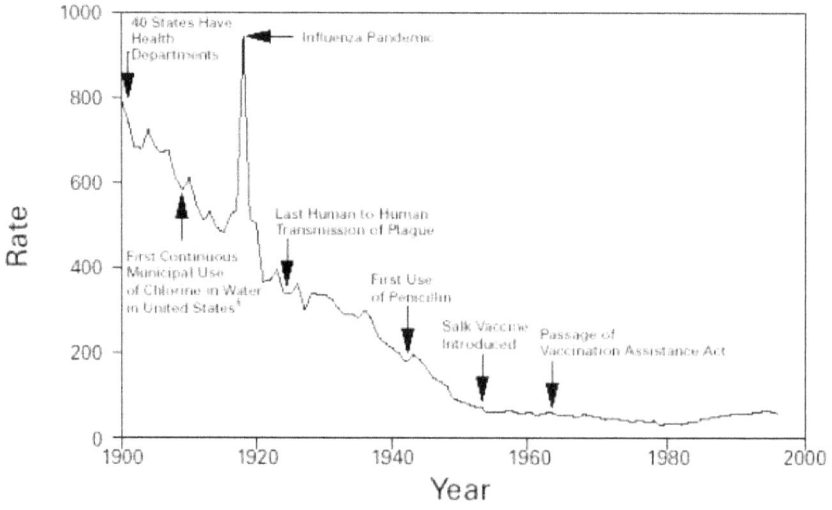

Source: Center for Disease Control.

The Ford assembly line transformed productivity in the auto industry and made the car affordable for the masses. The introduction of a moving assembly line into the auto industry by Henry Ford in 1913 materially increased the productivity of workers and lowered the cost of cars for the public. Ford's assembly line helped reduce the time required to produce a Model T from over twelve hours to under two hours. Supported by these productivity gains, Ford was able to reduce the cost of producing a Model T and lowered prices by over 50 percent. For the first time, the car, previously regarded as an exclusive product for the very wealthy in society, became affordable for the middle class (and for Ford assembly-line employees, who were able to earn more due to their higher productivity). Auto production in the United States increased rapidly—from thousands of units per year before the invention to millions of units every year. By 1920, auto production in the United States exceeded two million units a year and Ford produced over half of these units.

Figure 2.2. The Ford Assembly Line (1913)

Source: Ford Motor

The rapid development of the global auto industry, based on Ford's assembly-line innovation, had a strong ripple effect across several other industries. It stimulated the growth of a significant number of new industries and created a large number of jobs in the process. The requirement for insurance supported the development of a large auto-insurance industry (creating jobs for insurance underwriters, salespeople and claims processors). The growing number of auto manufacturers and cars supported the development of auto dealerships and the auto-servicing industry. The mass adoption of cars has been the major growth driver of the petroleum industry. Growing requirements for accessories and safety features supports the development of many subindustries in auto supplies. The building of public highways, a major investment to improve travel time, had ripple effects of its own, producing a significant number of direct jobs and much more. By improving the efficiency of road travel, the highway increased demand for moving goods by trucks and supported the growth of truck manufacturing and servicing and other related industries. The auto industry is a highly competitive industry with a strong consumer focus. It spends billions of dollars every year on advertising to entice consumers with new features (a major boost to the advertising industry). Higher levels of affordability for cars have enabled the growth of the suburban housing industry all around the world. The moving assembly line innovation at Ford was later adopted by the broad manufacturing industry and has contributed to gains in manufacturing productivity and increased consumer affordability for a wide range of products.

Innovation in agricultural technology has improved food security and freed up human capital resources to create value in other fields. Innovation in agriculture machinery and technology (tractors, higher yielding seeds, fertilizers, advances in soil science, and pest control techniques) has made it possible to increase food production with fewer and fewer farmworkers. In the eighteen hundreds, the majority of the US population worked in agriculture. Today, less than two percent of the US population work on farms, but overall agricultural production has risen over time. The adoption of these productivity enhancing innovations in developing countries, is transforming what were once nations of farmers in Latin America, Africa, India, and China, into nations with a declining number of farmers and a growing number of factory workers, software engineers, doctors, and people employed in the service industry. Productivity gains in agriculture have freed up labour resources for other productive uses and created employment growth, greater diversity in economic activity, rising wage levels and higher living standards around the world.

Innovation in household technology in the form of washing machines, dishwashers, microwaves, and vacuum cleaners has reduced the amount of time required to do household chores. Improvements in manufacturing productivity have lowered the cost of these products and supported mass adoption around the world. Over the past decades, increased productivity in domestic chores has facilitated greater economic participation and employment opportunities for women in all countries.

Innovation in air and sea travel has lowered the cost of communication and transportation and facilitated global trade. Affordability, comfort, and travel time have improved considerably over time. Productivity gains in air and sea travel have made it possible for firms to expand and manage businesses across many countries. Efficient air and sea travel has facilitated greater economic and social interaction around the world.

Innovation in computer technology and the Internet has improved productivity levels in the economy and supported the growth of new industries. Innovation in computer technology has triggered an exponential decline in the cost of computer devices and encouraged mass adoption. Moore's Law, described in 1965 by Gordon

Moore (cofounder of Intel), boils down to the observation that the cost of a given amount of computing power falls by half every eighteen months. In other words, over the same period the amount of computing power available at a particular price doubles. Over time, this exponential decline in the cost of computing power has supported high levels of adoption. Accessible and affordable computing power is driving rising productivity for businesses, governments, and individuals by enabling more efficient information gathering, processing, and sharing.

E-commerce is one of many new industries that has emerged from advances in computer technology. Growing computing power at affordable prices makes it possible for online retailers to manage and monitor inventory levels at a much lower cost. By connecting directly to the consumer via the Internet, online retailers provide increased convenience to the consumer and avoid the cost of maintaining physical presence in expensive shopping areas. E-commerce has raised productivity levels in the retail industry. Its lower cost structure encourages creativity and innovation from a greater number of individual and small business suppliers. These suppliers may lack the large capital resources required to have a physical presence in central shopping areas. The e-commerce industry has meaningfully increased consumer choice, lowered prices, and made the shopping experience more convenient and efficient. E-commerce is also removing location driven limits to a consumer's shopping experience.

Advances in mobile phone technology have contributed to considerable gains in personal productivity. Today, for social and entertainment functions, a mobile phone provides a more convenient and efficient alternative to a number of large and expensive gadgets such as traditional stand-alone cameras, radios, and cd players. With a smart mobile phone, it is now possible to surf the web, make phone calls, e-mail, access a variety of entertainment sources (movies, TV, music, and books), make reservations for hotels and restaurants, and access a global or national shopping experience from virtually anywhere.

COMPETITION SUPPORTS ECONOMIC GROWTH
BY CREATING STRONG INCENTIVES FOR VALUE CREATION

Private businesses are established with a goal of maximizing profits. Competition is the essential ingredient that makes it possible for the profit seeking motives of firms to lead to an improvement in public welfare. When there is little or no competition, a firm can abuse its cozy position or market power to serve the interests of shareholders at the expense of its customers. When firms have the power to influence prices, they often use that power to set prices substantially above the cost of resources employed in production and earn large profits at the expense of the general public. Competition reduces a firm's market power, supports "fair" prices (that reflect the cost of production), and expands consumer choice.

Competition is the vital element that aligns the interests of consumers with the profit seeking motives of firms.

By connecting financial rewards to value creation, competition creates a merit-based incentive system that stimulates innovation and productivity. Innovation and productivity gains lead to the production of more valuable goods at affordable prices. Competition assigns power to consumers to independently reward producers that deliver the most value in the form of higher quality products at lower prices. In a competitive market, consumers have choice, and a firm's ability to sell products has to be earned by creating value for consumers. Firms that sell the most products or earn the most attractive financial rewards are those that create the most value for their customers. The potential to earn extraordinary profits is not tied to political connections, special relationships, or favourable legislation, and it is not permanent. In a competitive market, the winners or beneficiaries of the most attractive financial rewards are constantly changing to reward firms and workers that are delivering the most value at any given point in time. This merit-based system of rewarding value creation sends strong signals to all economic participants to invest in innovation and productivity initiatives that ultimately support economic growth and higher living standards.

In competitive markets, financial rewards are linked to productivity gains, and the whole society benefits from stronger productivity incentives. To further illustrate this point, consider a country that has only one shoe manufacturer (and let's assume that there is no trade with other countries). A market dominated by a single producer limits consumer choice. In an effort to increase its profits, the shoe manufacturer could decide to raise prices or lower the quality of shoes at the expense of consumers. At higher prices, consumers can afford to buy fewer shoes, and production falls. When there is no competition, a producer may achieve its profit growth objectives at the expense of the general public by offering low quality goods at high prices. Furthermore, because a dominant firm can abuse its market power to increase profits, it has few incentives to invest in productivity enhancing technology or employee productivity initiatives. Without competition, the profit-maximizing goals of firms may work against improving the welfare of the general public.

Competitive markets create a win-win situation between members of the public and firms that create the most value. In a competitive industry, a firm can only earn high levels of profits (relative to its peers) when it creates more value for society.

In a competitive market for shoemaking, there are a large number of producers. Each producer devotes a considerable amount of effort to attract the attention of consumers. Firms that deliver the most attractive price-quality offerings generate larger revenue and profits. In such an environment, a shoe manufacturer is likely to take greater interest in technology that has the potential to lower the cost of producing shoes. With a lower cost of production, a shoe manufacturer can sell more shoes at lower prices but may still earn high profits. The difference this time is that, high profits are earned through the creation of greater value for consumers (higher production and lower prices). A manufacturer makes more money than competitors only by offering a superior price-quality proposition to customers.

In a competitive market, a manufacturer is rewarded for producing quality products at a lower cost; the manufacturer is therefore more likely to create incentives that encourage employee productivity. For example, in a competitive market, a shoe manufacturer is more likely to link employee wages to the number of shoes they are able to produce over a given period. When productivity is rewarded, employees have stronger incentives to invest time and effort in developing skills that enable them to create more value i.e. produce more and create higher quality products. Employees who earn higher wages compared to their peers do so because they are creating more value for society (more affordable and higher quality shoes).

Perhaps the most powerful feature of competitive markets is the value-creating signals they send through the economy. These have the potential to create a positive feedback loop that encourages all firms to continually seek opportunities to improve and deliver greater value for society. The large profits a shoe manufacturer earns by investing in productivity-enhancing technology and business processes sends signals to other shoe manufacturers to adopt productivity-enhancing initiatives in their efforts to maximize their own profits. The net effect is that, the desire to innovate and improve becomes endemic across all firms, and workers in the economy and the general public can benefit from structural improvements in quality and affordability over time.

Competition creates merit based incentives that can support a virtuous circle of innovation and productivity and lead to sustainable improvement in living standards.

Competition creates merit-based incentives that extend beyond product markets. Competition in capital markets supports the channeling of financial resources to companies that have the most attractive investment opportunities and profit prospects. This creates value for society because, in a competitive market, attractive profit-growth prospects can only be sustained by firms that create the most value for their customers. Competitive financial markets withdraw capital from the least efficient firms that do not generate sufficient revenue to cover the cost of resources employed in production. A competitive labour market better connects employee financial compensation (wages) with productivity levels (within a skill category) and creates stronger incentives for individuals to invest resources to improve their skills. Healthy competition in the political process creates more opportunities for voters to make informed decisions and has the potential to improve governance standards.

Competition democratizes economic decision making and improves social welfare. Without competition, social welfare is unlikely to be maximized in the market for most products. Regulatory bodies that are interested in promoting public welfare should enact policies that encourage competition. Such policies put the interest of the public ahead of the interest of a limited number of firms, and they create greater opportunities for economic progress.

When the government becomes a key provider of services that can be supplied by the private sector, it stifles competition, reduces consumer choice, and may restrict economic progress. The government has superior legal powers and greater financial resources than private citizens. This makes it very difficult (if not impossible) for private citizens to compete fairly against the government. Furthermore, when state owned enterprises have dominant positions in key sectors of the economy, the government may be less able to promote the welfare of consumers. The power of competition to promote innovation and drive down cost has been so impressive that many governments are finding more opportunities to encourage competition in the provision of public services. Sectors such as utilities and telecommunications that were once widely monopolized by governments have been opened up for competition in many countries. The US government's space agency, NASA, has recently started to encourage private competition for some of its space programs and is already experiencing significant gains in cost improvement and innovation in space travel. Space research is at the extreme end of a number of services that have historically been under exclusive government control (with zero competition) because of national security concerns. If it is possible to have some competition in space travel and research, there is perhaps far greater scope for competition in the delivery of public services than may be currently appreciated.

High levels of competition create considerable benefits for the general public. But powerful firms are not big fans of competition, because it requires them to work harder for profits. Governments may need to intervene to protect public interest when powerful firms take action to reduce competition. When firms have excessive market power, it may be necessary for the government to intervene to increase the level of competition in a particular industry to promote public welfare. Some industries require a considerable amount of capital. Consequently, these industries may only be able to attract and sustain a few producers in a country. Especially in low-income countries or countries with small populations, such industries typically have a few dominant national players who often have strong political connections. In such cases, opening up for international trade may present a viable route to greater competition. The deeper level of competition enabled by global trade intensifies the pace of innovation and productivity gains.

In order to create conditions for true competition, the ability of any firm (or number of firms acting together) to influence market prices and control consumer choice has to be limited.

When there is little or no competition, firms are more likely to maximize their profits at the expense of the general public. Firms may attempt to collude in setting prices or combine forces (through a merger) in order to stifle competition and increase their market power. When companies have excessive market power, their profit-seeking motive can lead them to abuse public trust and take unfair advantage of their customers. Excessive market power can also generate unhealthy levels of political influence and distort economic and social incentives in a country. In order to maintain healthy levels of competition, the ability of a firm to influence market prices and control consumer choice has to be limited.

In extreme cases of market power, in the interest of protecting and improving social welfare, it may be necessary to employ government regulation to break up excessively large and influential firms. For example, the US Supreme Court voted to break up Standard Oil in 1922 and AT&T in the early eighties, two of the largest and most powerful companies in their respective eras, in order to stimulate competition in oil refining and distribution (in the case of Standard Oil) and telecommunications (in the case of AT&T). At one stage, Standard Oil controlled 90% of crude refining capacity in the United States. It abused its market power by charging high prices in regions where it faced little competition. In regions where it faced greater competitive treats, Standard Oil charged unreasonably low prices in order to discourage new competitors from expanding. Ending AT&T's monopoly over telecommunication services resulted in much lower long distance call rates in the United States. In many countries, the ability of firms to collude to set prices is illegal. In order to promote public welfare, firms may be required to seek approval from dedicated government agencies, before acquiring or merging with other firms.

3

INTERNATIONAL TRADE AND GLOBALIZATION
THE CONSUMER'S FRIEND

The extension and use of railroads, steamships, telegraphs, break down nationalities and bring peoples geographically remote into close connection commercially and politically. They make the world one, and capital, like water, tends to a common level.
—David Livingstone, missionary and explorer (1813-73).

High levels of interest in voluntary exchange among individuals support the view that trade and globalization have the potential to create value for all parties involved. Even when an individual has the necessary skills to earn a wage from a profession, bake his own bread, grow his own food, and sew his own clothes, he still finds it prudent to specialize in some of these activities (typically the ones that generate higher value or income) and use his income to purchase goods that other people produce. We all engage in trade every day of our lives. We trade our skills and time for jobs to earn income and trade our wages for houses, food, clothes and other desirable products. If a person was to restrict his consumption only to those goods that he was capable of producing, this would grossly limit his quality of life. If a country restricted the consumption of its citizens and businesses to goods produced within its borders, living standards may be much lower than income levels can afford if trade with other countries was possible. Greater opportunities for exchange have the potential to increase consumption possibilities and improve the well-being of people in all countries.

Case Study 3.1.

All Countries Have the Potential to Benefit from International Trade Irrespective of Their Productive Abilities

Imagine a world where there are two deadly diseases (A and B) affecting every country. After years of research, an effective drug for disease A was found in one country, and a drug for disease B was found in a different country. Even after this initial success with drugs, trade is necessary to improve the well-being of all citizens in the world. Without trade, people in all countries will remain vulnerable to the threat of these diseases. Even for those countries that have developed effective drugs, the health of citizens cannot be fully improved without trade. By trading with the rest of the world, countries with drugs can earn additional income and improve the health of their citizens. Trading with the rest of the world creates more value than restricting trade to nations that have developed effective drugs. For countries that have not developed the capability to produce either drug, opportunities to buy drugs from other countries are priceless. Trade increases revenue growth opportunities for firms that create value for their customers. By trading with the rest of the world, the pharmaceutical companies responsible for developing these drugs can command greater financial resources to support drug research and production expansion. These, in turn, can potentially lead to the creation of more effective drugs at lower prices for all global citizens.

The key message from this story applies to many products in the real world that have the potential to create significant value for global citizens but may only be produced in a few countries. For example, Boeing and Airbus (in the United States and in Europe) are the only two companies that have the technology and capability to competitively produce large, long-haul commercial airplanes. Through international trade, all countries are able to extract great benefits from these products. Through their purchasing decisions, customers around the world are indirectly contributing towards funding research and productivity enhancement initiatives of these firms, which may eventually lower the cost of travel for all global citizens (e.g. through the development of fuel efficient airplanes).

*****

Globalization refers to the broader level of economic and social interaction between nations to facilitate trade, share information and best ideas, and promote greater cooperation in dealing with economic, social, and political challenges around the world. Globalization promotes healthy competition and cooperation between nations with the ultimate goal of raising living standards of people in all countries. Globalization has the potential to enable the creation of larger and more efficient markets for goods and services. It has the potential to reduce political uncertainty and promote global peace. Globalization enables the ultimate form of economic democracy; it allows individuals to maximize the value of their income and businesses to maximize their opportunities for investment across a wider range of possibilities. Healthy competition for capital and investment between countries as well as greater opportunities for political interaction can support higher economic growth and better governance standards around the world.

SOME KEY ADVANTAGES OF GLOBALIZATION

Globalization breaks down geographic limits to sharing ideas (the neighbourhood effect) by creating a platform that promotes the adoption of best practices without regard to country borders. By creating an open platform for trade, political cooperation, and greater interaction, globalization allows for sharing best practices on governance, institution building, technology and business management techniques to enhance productivity and living standards around the world.

The high cost of transportation and communication has historically placed geographic limits on economic and political interaction among nations. In the past, many countries enjoyed strong economic ties only with their neighbours. Traditionally, when a country achieved major strides in economic growth via new technological innovations, such new ideas were transmitted primarily to their neighbours. Due to the historically strong neighbourhood effect, it is not surprising that even today, the geographic location of a country is a key determinant of productivity levels and living standards. The most productive countries (i.e., high-income countries) tend to be clustered around each other, while the least productive countries (low-income countries) are often concentrated in particular regions. The level of political stability within nations appears to also largely depend on their geographic locations. The behavior and economic prospects of a country's neighbour has been overly influential in determining its own prospects.

Globalization removes geographic limits on sharing ideas; it improves upon the quality of the neighborhood effect by creating a much deeper pool of best practices from which any country can choose. Globalization is providing opportunities to promote human progress beyond the limits set by country borders. However, the degree to which a country benefits from globalization largely depends on its ability to proactively take advantage of this platform for greater interaction.

Two shining examples of how globalization has enabled countries to escape weak neighbourhood effects to embrace new ideas from other parts of the world to improve living standards.

1. **Political stability becomes a reality in Africa**. In many African nations, there has been a dramatic improvement in political stability since the early nineties. Global political and economic support for democracy on the continent has been instrumental in aiding the transformation of traditionally unstable military governments into stable democracies. Within two decades, democracy appears to have taken root in Africa. Political stability is stimulating economic growth by encouraging local and foreign investment. Growing political stability has helped many African nations to sustain robust economic growth rates and strong gains in living standards over the past decade.

2. **Without technology leadership, China leapfrogs to become the global leader in e-commerce.** Advances in computer technology have helped some emerging market countries (late starters) to leapfrog into leadership positions in productivity by tapping into global best practices. For example, in 2000, China had a few million Internet users and no major e-commerce (online retail and trade) companies. By 2013, China had 600 million Internet users, and its e-commerce market overtook that of the United States to become the largest in the world. E-commerce provides a more cost-effective and convenient way of shopping and trading, which stimulates greater innovation and productivity in

the retail industry. Jack Ma, the founder and chairman of China's Alibaba (the largest and the most valuable e-commerce company in the world in 2014) is attributed with saying that while e-commerce may only provide another way of shopping in more developed countries, in China it is a lifestyle. In 2014, Alibaba facilitated over $350 billion worth of transactions on its e-commerce websites. This was far greater than the combined value of transactions on Amazon and eBay (pioneers in the global ecommerce industry). Chinese e-commerce companies and Chinese consumers have capitalized on leading global innovations to develop the most advanced and most productive shopping and retail experience in the world.

Globalization provides opportunities to promote human progress beyond limits set by country borders. However, the degree to which a country benefits from globalization largely depends on its ability to take advantage of this platform for greater interaction. Chinese companies have not (yet) been key players in mobile-phone technology innovation. They were not instrumental in pioneering the smartphone or the e-commerce industry. However, by proactively tapping into globally available technology innovations, companies like Alibaba have been able to create the most advanced shopping experiences for Chinese consumers and the most productive retail opportunities for Chinese businesses.

*****

Globalization supports the development of local businesses with productivity enhancing ideas and technology. By creating a strong platform for interaction, globalization provides an effective transmission mechanism for best ideas developed in local industries in one part of the world to penetrate other countries. A large proportion of all goods and services produced in any country is primarily targeted at the local market. Services such as education, banking, healthcare, catering, construction, and retail are primarily local industries that do not compete in global markets. Through globalization, local businesses can extract process and equipment innovations and other best practices developed in other parts of the world to improve the quality of local services. High-income countries may have larger financial resources to fund research efforts and productivity enhancing initiatives in many industries. A country may focus its research efforts in specific sectors that are more relevant for its economy. Through greater global interaction, any country can share research findings and technology innovations with the rest of the world. For example, the sharing of information about discoveries in medicine and crop science has been instrumental in lifting the quality of agricultural and medical services in many countries. The spread of information about productivity enhancing technologies in supply chain management and logistics is helping to improve the efficiency of manufacturing and retail activities around the world. Opportunities to access productivity enhancing technology may support local businesses to create more value for local residents, and in some cases, may help create new industries and services.

By creating a larger market for products, globalization intensifies the level of competition and stimulates innovation and productivity gains. This translates into continual improvement in product quality and lower prices for consumers in all countries. In the global marketplace, consumers have access to a wide variety of products from suppliers all over the world. Their purchasing decisions are guided by an interest in seeking the best value for their money without much consideration of the identities of the producers or where goods are produced. In the global market, greater opportunities for consumer choice signal to producers that consumers are only loyal to suppliers that deliver the most desirable products at the most compelling prices. Greater competition provides stronger incentives for producers to continually innovate in order to deliver more value for consumers.

The global marketplace presents opportunities as well as challenges for producers. In order to benefit from this large but more competitive market place, producers have to constantly invest to improve their production practices and continuously innovate to deliver attractive products at compelling prices. Dominant national champions become smaller players in a much larger and more competitive globalized market, and they are pressured to be more responsive to consumer demands, lest they risk losing business.

The global marketplace magnifies potential gains for producers that deliver the most value (in quality and price), but it equally magnifies potential losses for producers whose products fail to live up to consumer expectations. The larger market size makes it more feasible for companies to invest significant amounts of resources in technology and other productivity enhancing techniques in order to improve product quality and lower the cost of production. To stay relevant as a supplier to the global market, a producer has to be able to lead in innovation and respond to product innovation elsewhere, or the producer may lose out to more dynamic and efficient competitors. While some producers win and others lose, the global consumer always wins. International trade pressures local industries to champion the cause of local citizens by truly delivering value comparable to what those citizens can obtain in the global market. The global market has the potential to eliminate situations where dominant local firms can abuse their market power to increase profitability at the expense of local consumers.

Globalization in trade means that the best products, in any given industry, are available to consumers in all countries and are produced by employing the most efficient resources. Global trade encourages greater competition by creating larger financial rewards for producers who deliver desirable products at the most compelling prices. To stay competitive, firms have to take advantage of the most efficient suppliers of components and the most cost effective places to manufacture products.

Some firms or countries have developed competitive advantages that make them more efficient at producing certain goods. A competitive advantage may develop as a result of technology leadership that may not be available to other suppliers. Firms in some countries may enjoy a cost advantage in producing certain goods because of the availability of cheap raw materials and other resources (e.g. cheap labour). In some industries, the cost of production has the potential to fall substantially when goods are produced in very large quantities. Global markets intensify the benefits of such scale advantages and may lead to a concentration of production within a few efficient firms in order to lower product prices for all global consumers. Without these competitive advantages, a country may not have the technology to produce certain products or may only be able to produce at a much higher cost. By taking advantage of the most competitive producers around the world, global trade raises the efficiency of production and shares the gains among all global consumers.

The intense level of competition in global trade has pushed companies beyond the boundaries of their own countries in search of greater efficiency and scale. Today, hardly any product is 100 percent made by one firm or in one country. To stay competitive, each producer looks around the world to see where he can source each component at the most competitive price. Most global manufacturers are increasingly truly global with respect to how they source their inputs, where they manufacture, and where they sell their products. As globalization intensifies, the idea of a "Made in country X" tag on a product loses significance. Just as buyers for these products have become global, employees, suppliers, production facilities, and providers of capital have also become more global in nature.

Global sports such as football showcase the power of global markets in promoting merit-based incentives and continual improvement in product quality. Football fans are spread across the globe, and they demand high quality football. High levels of competition in football ensure meritocracy in the selection of players and coaches. The top football clubs may be based in Europe, but positions for players and coaches are filled by the best candidates from all over the world. Notwithstanding strong political pressure to support the development of local talent, the composition of many top teams is no longer representative of where the teams are located. Globalization of the game has also expanded the resources available to these teams to deliver a superior product for all global consumers than would be possible if the market was restricted to local fans and local players. In order to enjoy international football of the highest quality that features the best players in the world, football fans no longer have to wait four years for the World Cup. This highly desirable product is now available on a weekly basis.

Local production can retain strong advantages in a global market. Local production reduces transportation cost, improves the ability of producers to adapt to changes in local consumer tastes, and typically enjoys preferential tax terms when compared to imported goods. Competitive global firms often have local production facilities in countries where they have a large number of customers, in order to take advantage of some of these benefits.

The auto industry is a highly competitive global industry that retains several advantages of local production. For example, the large US car market attracts many global producers. As of 2014, Asian car producers such as Toyota, Nissan, Honda, Kia, and Hyundai had an over 40 percent combined market share in the United States. Because of strong local advantages in auto assembly, Asian auto companies have built manufacturing plants in the United States that primarily employ American workers. In a similar fashion, Ford and General Motors (the two largest US producers) generate 40 to

50 percent of their total sales from international markets and have local manufacturing presence across several countries in key markets such as Europe and Asia. In highly competitive product markets, local production is only undertaken for components or specific stages in the production process that enjoy strong local advantages. Toyota will only locate a car assembly plant in the U.S. (or any other country) when it the least costly place to assemble cars for than market. For cars produced in the US, key components may still be sourced from more efficient suppliers in other countries.

Coca-Cola, a global soft drink brand was established in Atlanta, Georgia, United States in 1886. Today, it is one of the largest global brands. On any given day, up to two billion servings of Coca-Cola products are delivered around the world. Coca-Cola may be widely perceived to be an American company, but its operations and value creation are potentially more local. The Coca-Cola Company has bottling plants in almost every country. Coca-Cola products available in any country are truly locally manufactured products. The bottling plants are operated by local employees, and the company pays taxes to local governments on behalf of employees and on profits derived from local operations. Coca-Cola owns the brand and sells concentrate to these operations, but all other inputs such as sugar, water, aluminum, and plastics, are either sourced locally or from other globally competitive producers. The entire Coca-Cola distribution system, made up of a large fleet of trucks, wholesale distributors, supermarkets, restaurants, and small shops is local and generates a significant number of jobs in many countries. When one considers the full value chain of Coca-Cola, it becomes clear that while the brand may be global, most of the key stages involved in making Coca-Cola one of the most successful consumer products are local.

Globalization increases the production possibilities of the world. The larger addressable market created by globalization provides greater resources for product development and may support the production of goods that might not be viable if demand were restricted to national markets. For some goods, the unit cost of production can fall significantly when goods are produced in very large quantities (economies of scale). The quantities involved may be larger than the demand for those goods in certain countries such that without global trade, some countries may be denied access to certain goods or may have to pay prohibitively high prices for them.

For example, globalization in the entertainment industry (music, movies, and sports) increases access to a wider variety of quality entertainment at competitive prices. A global market increases the scope to produce a wider range of entertainment because it spreads the significant investment involved across a larger number of consumers. The massive spending power of the global entertainment industry supports innovation in equipment and techniques that eventually become available to local producers at a fraction of the original cost. With greater access to superior technology, local producers can increase the quality of local content for greater consumer satisfaction. There are a large number of specialized products (e.g., drug research on rare diseases) that would not be viable (even in high-income countries) without the larger demand opportunities available from globalization. A number of expensive productivity enhancing techniques that help to improve product quality and lower the cost of consumer goods (e.g. the use of robots in auto assembly) may not be viable outside of the large market that globalization enables.

The gains from globalization have been experienced by consumers in every country. The gains from globalization can be seen in the rising quality and affordability of cars, computers, microwaves, and many other consumer products that were once regarded as luxury products even in the most productive nations (i.e. high-income countries).

Extensive access to immense productivity gains in mobile phone technology helps to illustrate the power of global trade to improve living standards for consumers in every corner of the world. The first commercially available mobile phone, the Motorola DynaTAC was released in the early eighties at a price of four thousand dollars, about nine thousand dollars in 2014 prices when adjusted for inflation. The phone (nicknamed the "Brick") was large and heavy and could only be used for thirty minutes before the battery died. The price of the phone was equivalent to a quarter of the average annual salary in the United States and was out of the reach of most American consumers, let alone poor, rural consumers in developing countries who may live on a few dollars of income per day. The large global addressable market for mobile phones encouraged competition, investment, and product innovation that eventually drove down prices and improved product quality. Over time, the compounded effect of innovation and productivity gains has improved the functionality of the mobile phone and driven prices to such low levels that consumers in the poorest countries in the world have become regular users of mobile phone technology. In a number of developing countries, many people still do not have reliable access to basic utility services such as piped water and electricity, which are provided by local authorities. However, because they are part of a global market in communication and computer technology, they are able to share the gains of innovation and efficiency improvement just like all other consumers. By being part of the global market, their consumption possibilities are not limited by local capabilities.

RESISTANCE TO GLOBALIZATION

Within the same country, ordinary people freely trade their resources with neighbours and strangers alike, in order to improve their well-being. However, throughout history, governments have often taken steps to restrict international trade, and public opinion can sometimes be skeptical about the benefits of globalization, particularly in trade.

Even when economic gains from globalization far exceed economic losses, there may be large and undesirable social costs associated with the economic losses. The process of generating productivity gains from global trade may create job losses for industries and firms that are not able to compete. When a large number of job losses are involved, the potentially high social cost (unemployment and poverty) associated with such losses could reduce public interest in global trade. The gains from globalization are spread among an entire population, but job losses are often concentrated and more obvious in particular firms or regions and may therefore attract far greater public attention and political interest even when the proportion of jobs lost (relative to the total employment base in a country) is minimal.

Broader education about the diverse and long-term potential gains from globalization may be necessary to maintain public support. Global trade can bring about job losses in one sector of the economy, but it also has the potential to create new employment opportunities in other sectors. Even when a country is not an active seller into the global marketplace, globalization has the potential to create significant long-term benefits. Large cost savings on some internationally sourced products, compared to what it would cost to produce them locally, and greater access to productivity enhancing technology can support job creation in diverse parts of an economy. For example, steel and cement producers in many countries cry out for government protection (in the form of higher taxes on imports and other subsidies) against international producers whenever international prices are much lower than domestic prices. When international prices are substantially lower than local prices, trading with the rest of the world may force local producers to improve their productivity or shut down inefficient plants. Even in a worst-case scenario, where local producers shut down, global trade can still generate value and job creation in other parts of the economy. For example, significant cost savings on imported steel or cement could stimulate higher investment activity in construction and real-estate development. Higher levels of real-estate activity could support the creation of a far greater number of jobs (compared to jobs lost in steel or cement production) directly in construction, real-estate sales and marketing, home and office improvement, and indirectly in activities that cheaper construction cost enables such as retail and local business expansion. Furthermore, by fostering greater interaction, globalization can enable local businesses to access the most advanced productivity enhancing technology and processes to improve the range and quality of local services. Greater value creation in local services can help expand employment opportunities.

The main challenge of globalization is that of reallocating labour resources from an industry that loses competitiveness to other areas of the economy where new opportunities are being created. Rather than stifle global trade, benefits could be maximized at a lower cost if governments increased global awareness within education platforms, put in place effective job and skill training programs to help create a more adaptable workforce, and provide adequate compensation (income support) for inevitable job losses. However, the ability to reallocate labour resources to more productive areas of the economy could be constrained in countries that have structurally high levels of unemployment.

Governments may need to protect local industries when there is a high social cost associated with losing competitiveness or where young industries have the potential to become globally competitive. To champion the welfare of all citizens in the long term, a government may need to introduce temporary trade barriers (e.g., higher taxes on imported goods or some subsidies) in cases where the social cost of job losses could be immense, or in situations where young industries have the potential to compete globally but lack the necessary scale and investment to be competitive in the short-term. Temporary trade barriers and targeted financial support can encourage investment in local industries to raise productivity levels towards global standards.

Permanent trade barriers or predictable government intervention whenever local producers feel threatened by more productive global suppliers, may reduce incentives for local industries to improve. Permanent trade barriers work against the welfare of the general public, because they are effectively a form of long-term tax on citizens to support inefficient local industries. For example, the global steel industry is highly competitive and profit margins are thin for most producers. However, historically, supported by government protection mechanism, steel producers in Brazil and India have been able to enjoy high profit margins at the expense of local consumers. In both countries a small number of steel producers dominate the industry and have been able to take advantage of their market power to charge higher prices than consumers can access on global markets. Steel producers in these countries have been successful in protecting their high profit margins from global competition by lobbying their governments to raise taxes on imports. The net effect is that, industrial manufacturers and other users of steel in Brazil and India pay higher prices for steel and may be less competitive as a result. High levels of government protection in the steel industry, where producers are concentrated and enjoy a high level of political influence, may ultimately result in lower levels of employment opportunities in local manufacturing industries (relative to their potential).

Trade barriers are most costly in situations where there is either no domestic production capacity or where demand for a product rises far beyond the production capacity of local producers. Rising demand and restricted supply can cause prices to rise sharply and reduce consumption, investment, and economic growth relative to potential. The economic gains that local producers earn from higher prices may be much smaller than the overall economic losses that the general public is likely to suffer.

GLOBALIZATION OF FINANCIAL MARKETS

With rising interaction among countries, capital providers (savers) have greater opportunities to access the most financially rewarding investments. The opportunity to invest in international markets has the potential to enhance the returns of capital providers and increase the diversification of their investments. Globalization of financial markets provides access to investment opportunities in industries that may not exist in one's home country. The mobility of funds on a global scale creates stronger competition among governments and businesses for capital. Greater competition for capital in a global market, favours the most productive and innovative businesses that deliver value for their customers and governments that pursue prudent economic policies. In countries with low savings rates (low supply of capital), globalization of financial markets makes it possible for governments and businesses to finance attractive investment opportunities by accessing funds from international investors.

Domestic Bias. Globalization creates economic efficiencies, drives innovation, and improves affordability of products. However in some instances there may be a behavioural or cultural preference for locally produced goods and local investments. Globalization may be well entrenched in consumer product markets, but financial markets still exhibit high degrees of domestic bias. For example, while Toyota is one of the best-selling car brands in the United States, American investors may be more likely to provide capital to Ford and General Motors than Toyota. To access funds for investment, many companies restrict themselves to local banks rather than tap into international bond markets. Globalization in financial markets is growing but lags behind what has been achieved in product markets. A key reason for the strong preference of domestic investments is that government policies can often have a considerable impact on the value of investments. International investors have no voting power in foreign countries and may face a higher level of political and economic risks when investing abroad.

GLOBALIZATION INCREASES ECONOMIC INTERDEPENDENCE

Through globalization, the economic prospects of countries have become more interdependent. It may no longer be possible to assess a country's economic performance in isolation. A country's economic growth potential is not influenced by local-demand conditions exclusively. With greater economic interaction, global factors may play a meaningful role. In periods of rising economic growth and investment demand in large economies, the higher demand for capital and commodity resources has the potential to raise the level of interest rates and commodity prices around the world. When a major buyer of a product on the global market has economic difficulties and begins to buy less than usual, major producers of that product may also feel the pain. Alternatively, when a major buyer of a product on the global market is experiencing strong economic growth, the higher global demand fuels strong wealth effects for countries and businesses that supply the product. Countries that derive large revenue and employment from exporting manufactured goods or commodities and those that are heavily dependent on international sources of capital are likely to be affected most by changes in global demand conditions.

Elected governments often take credit for periods of strong economic growth but blame economic challenges on deteriorating global conditions. However, due to growing economic interdependence between countries, it may not be prudent to evaluate the economic performance of a country or a government in isolation. A comparison of economic performance with other comparable countries (in a region or countries with a similar industry structure) may be more relevant.

For example, between 2001 and 2013, economic growth around the world was strongest for oil-producing nations (see figure 3.1). Rapid economic growth in China (a large economy with a population of over 1.3 billion) raised global demand for crude oil and other commodities. The price of a barrel of crude oil rose from thirty dollars in 2001 to one hundred dollars between 2010 and 2013. For oil-producing nations, the main driver of economic growth over this period has been the increase in oil prices, an externally driven factor. Therefore comparing economic growth rates between oil-producing countries may be more appropriate than comparing them to regional peers that do not produce oil. In general, countries that export natural resources benefitted immensely from rising demand in China during this period.

Figure 3.1. Countries with the Fastest $GDP Growth Rates in the World (2001 to 2013).

ranking out of 190 countries	Country	2013 GDP (US$, bn)	2013 GDP/Capita ($)	Annualized nominal ($) GDP growth rate 2001 to 2013	Main exports	Major source of Government Revenue
1	Angola	115	5,956	25.4%	Oil and gas	Oil and gas
2	Azerbaijan	69	8,165	24.1%	Oil and gas	Oil and gas
3	Timor-Leste	6	5,162	23.8%	Oil and gas	Oil and gas
4	Equatorial Guinea	18	22,344	23.1%	Oil and gas	Oil and gas
5	Qatar	192	104,655	22.5%	Oil and gas	Oil and gas
6	Iraq	213	6,377	22.1%	Oil and gas	Oil and gas
7	Kazakhstan	203	13,048	21.3%	Oil and gas	Oil and gas
8	Mongolia	10	3,881	19.9%	Mining	Mining
9	Tajikistan	8	1,050	19.0%	Oil and gas	Oil and gas
10	Myanmar	55	915	18.9%	Oil and gas	Oil and gas
11	Chad	13	1,234	17.6%	Oil and gas	Oil and gas
12	Russia	2,030	14,973	17.5%	Oil and gas	Oil and gas
13	China	8,221	6,569	17.2%	manufactured pdts	diverse
14	Nigeria	270	1,725	17.1%	Oil and gas	Oil and gas
15	Ghana	40	1,782	16.3%	Oil and Mining	Oil and Mining

Growth ranking for more diverse high-income countries over this period

136	Korea	1,198	23,838	7.5%
159	Germany	3,593	43,952	5.5%
172	United Kingdom	2,490	39,049	4.4%
176	United States	16,724	52,839	3.9%
186	Japan	5,007	39,321	1.6%

source: Author, IMF

4

DETERMINANTS OF EMPLOYMENT OPPORTUNITIES AND WAGE LEVELS IN THE ECONOMY

Jobs are relevant to all. Jobs help raise productivity, improve living standards, and promote social integration. Employment opportunities and "good jobs" that provide high levels of affordability are universally desired. Employment is a lifeline for individuals and households. Parents need the income from jobs in order to provide for themselves and their families. Parents invest in their children's education with the primary objective that children become economically independent adults. Employment creates greater opportunities for social engagement and helps to maintain high levels of self-esteem. Greater job opportunities increase the ability of people to pay taxes and support the provision of essential public services. A high level of unemployment is often associated with poverty, social unrest, and political instability. Unemployment and low wages are key economic challenges in many countries.

Formal education helps to develop important skills that can improve employment opportunities and wage prospects, but it does not guarantee the availability of jobs. Formal education increases opportunities for intellectual development and the acquisition of important skills that improves an employee's attractiveness to a potential employer. Attainment of higher levels of formal education and professional training can also send powerful signals to potential employers about a candidate's enthusiasm for learning and capacity to thrive under challenges. However, formal education does not guarantee adequate wage levels or the availability of jobs for appropriately skilled people. Education institutions are set up to provide learning opportunities; they do not always have an explicit aim of preparing people for the job market. Students and parents who see education as an important step towards employment need to take greater responsibility for how they utilize available education resources to improve their job prospects.

A passive investment in education may not yield optimal results in employment because it implicitly assumes that there are jobs available for all people who have attained high levels of formal education. In reality, the availability of jobs in any economy is primarily determined by the needs of businesses and governments that produce goods and provide services. Formal education helps to develop technical skills in specific disciplines as well as broader skills in work ethic, critical thinking, teamwork, and creativity. This broad set of skills has the ability to increase the productivity of formally educated employees and make them more valuable to firms. In a dynamic economy where skill requirements change over time, higher levels of formal education may also increase the ability of people to re-train for new job opportunities in the economy.

High levels of formal education improve the attractiveness of candidates to potential employers, but do not guarantee the availability of jobs. When employers (businesses and governments) are not able to create sufficient jobs in relation to the number of people available for work, there could be high levels of unemployment even for graduates with high education qualifications. A good understanding of the economy to identify sectors with structural growth opportunities can help young people tailor their skills development efforts and job search initiatives to improve their employment prospects. It is more practical for people to adapt their training and skills-development efforts to the types of jobs available in the economy than to hope for the economy or government policy to create jobs that fit their skills.

When employment is a clear goal for an investment in higher education, it may be more prudent to tailor skills development to available job opportunities than to assume that the economy will create jobs for all specialized skills acquired through higher education.

The quality of readily accessible job market information is generally poor. Proactive research to gather information about available employment opportunities and associated working conditions can generate potentially attractive rewards. The quality and availability of information on job opportunities and wage are generally poor. Typical sources of employment information such as newspaper ads, government employment agencies, university career centers, and company websites may not be representative of the range of employment opportunities available in the economy, and they often have incomplete information about working conditions and wages. The most extensive employment database or recruitment firm may only reflect a fraction of available job opportunities in an economy.

For competitive reasons, firms are generally not in favour of disclosing detailed information about job opportunities, wages, and working conditions, especially for highly skilled positions. Most employers consider wage contracts to be highly confidential. In some cases, firms may consider their hiring practices and wage policies to be a key differentiating factor that ought to be shielded from their competitors. Employees demand confidentiality on their wages and wage prospects. Due to the poor quality of readily accessible job-market information, one may only be able to access complete information about employment conditions and financial compensation well after one has gained employment. Due to these barriers, information about a large number of skilled positions are typically spread through informal networks such as friends and families of current employees and specialist recruitment agencies, without ever entering a broadly accessible public domain. Information barriers restrict the ability of people to make optimal investments in education and skills-training; they may further hinder people's ability to match skills to available job opportunities. In response to the high cost associated with job-market information barriers, specialist recruitment agencies and firms' human-resources departments play an important intermediary role between firms and employees by ensuring only selective disclosure of sensitive employment information.

Seeking greater information about the breadth of available employment opportunities may help people make more optimal decisions in their skills development choices. Jobs are essential and represent a major long-term incentive for an investment in education. Efforts to acquire detailed job-market information can be highly complementary to an investment in education or skills-training. Students, parents, and schools could be more proactive about building adequate levels of knowledge about employment opportunities in the economy. By networking through family and friends, taking internships (even when internships are without pay) across different industries, and taking full advantage of available career resources in schools and recruitment firms, individuals can materially increase their knowledge about job opportunities, wage prospects, and working conditions across different sectors of the economy.

An investment in higher education and skills training is costly. The return on this investment is more likely to be maximized when the investment decision is supported by extensive knowledge of potential job opportunities, wage prospects, and working conditions that can be enabled by such training.

UNEMPLOYMENT

There will always be some level of unemployment in the economy, because the process of searching for jobs or matching employee skills with available jobs takes time. People actively looking for jobs are considered to be unemployed. People of working age, who are neither currently employed, nor actively looking for jobs, are considered to be out of the job market rather than unemployed. Unemployment that arises because of the time required to match skills to available jobs is perhaps healthy, because a good match can improve productivity. In some cases, unemployment arises because of a shortage of workers with appropriate skills rather than a lack of job opportunities. When the skills demanded are easy to acquire in a timely manner, such employment opportunities are more realizable in the short-term. However, some skills may require several years of training, and the unemployment associated with such skills deficits could persist for some time. In many countries around the world, the most important challenge is the simple fact that there are not enough job opportunities in the economy for everyone willing to work. In other words, many countries have high levels of unemployment in most skill categories. The fundamental problem of job creation remains one of the major economic challenges in most countries and a key focus of government policy.

A healthy form of unemployment may arise as a result of the necessary time it takes to match employee skills to available job opportunities. Unemployment may also arise when there are not enough appropriately skilled workers for available jobs in the economy. Unemployment associated with a skills deficit, can be overcome with appropriate training. Unemployment arising from an inadequate number of job opportunities compared to the number of people available to work is the most challenging form of unemployment to resolve.

The economy is dynamic and requires a flexible and adaptable labour force. The process of economic growth requires the continual reallocation of resources (including labour resources) into more productive activities (away from less productive ones). The structure of every economy and its sources of job creation changes over time. This means that, at any given point, new jobs are created in some sectors of the economy while jobs are lost in other sectors. Some skills that were once highly sought after, may no longer be required in the future.

The dynamic nature of the economy requires a flexible and adaptable workforce. Labour laws that provide firms with the flexibility to hire workers in a timely manner and to lay off workers when their business prospects are less favourable ultimately increase the willingness of firms to hire, and can support higher levels of employment in an economy. When labour market regulations make it highly punitive and costly to lay off workers, employers become less willing to hire even when they can productively employ additional workers. The dynamism of the economy means that prospects are as uncertain for businesses as they are for employees. In order to remain competitive or survive, it may be crucial for firms to maintain the flexibility to adapt the quantity of resources employed (including labour) to changes in the economic environment.

To maximize their opportunities for employment, workers need to be flexible in their ability to adapt their training to new job opportunities in the economy. Greater opportunities for formal education and skills-training along with efficient platforms that disseminate up-to-date information about available job opportunities can help support the creation of a more adaptable workforce and potentially help improve employment levels in an economy. There is a significant difference in unemployment rates among countries with comparable economic structures and income levels. This suggests that some labour market policies and practices may be more conducive to job creation than others. A proactive approach by employees, firms, and governments to embrace and take advantage of the inevitable dynamism in the economy can support higher levels of job creation and employment.

To stay competitive and sustain current levels of employment, existing businesses have to be innovative to maintain their efficiency and product appeal. A business that does not invest to improve itself, is more likely to decline than stand still. Jobs and wages are only sustainable when the employer manages to preserve its ability to *create economic value*. A firm creates economic value when it is able to generate sufficient revenue to cover the cost of all resources employed in the production of goods or services. Employees need to understand how their employer creates economic value and be able to assess the economic prospects of their employer in order to determine the sustainability of their own jobs and wages. For example, a journalist needs to understand the connection between the quality of his writing to the success of his newspaper employer. He may also need to be aware of potential structural threats to newspaper readership due to the growing number of freely accessible media and entertainment opportunities via the Internet.

DETERMINANTS OF WAGE LEVELS AND EMPLOYMENT OPPORTUNITIES IN A COMPETITIVE LABOUR MARKET

In a competitive market, employers do not create jobs and raise wages as a welfare gesture. Neither do they derive any direct benefit from laying off workers or paying low wages. In a competitive market, a firm creates new jobs when hiring additional workers enables it to generate greater economic value in the form of higher production, sales, and profits. More specifically, the incremental economic value generated by hiring additional employees has to exceed or at least match the cost of hiring them. When the demand for a firm's products or services is on the rise, the firm may need to hire additional workers in order to increase production and sales. Under unfavourable demand conditions, when the sales and profit prospects of firms are poor, they are more likely to lay off workers in order to streamline their cost base to the lower production requirements.

With this in mind, an individual can significantly increase his employability and improve his wage prospects by understanding how his employer generates sales and profits and how he can contribute to this effort. A firm ultimately shares its revenue and profits among its stakeholders such as employees, suppliers, the government (in the form of taxes), and capital providers, and it may reinvest excess profits for growth. Employees that help their firms to produce more desirable goods at cost-competitive prices are more likely to earn higher wages for themselves and support the creation of new employment opportunities within their firms.

Employment opportunities and wage levels in an economy are determined by the type of value creating activities that businesses develop. In an economy where high levels of innovation help businesses to come up with desirable products and services, favourable prospects for sales and profit growth can support higher levels of employment and wages. When the products and services produced in an economy are less compelling due to low levels of innovation, businesses are more likely to experience limited growth prospects and create fewer jobs. Technological innovation has the potential to significantly increase the productivity of workers and can support higher wages and job creation. The auto industry is a major employer in many large economies and illustrates the job creation potential embedded in adding value to basic materials such as steel. Each layer of incremental value-add can create large employment opportunities.

A competitive job market for a particular skill helps to set wages at a level that supports higher employment opportunities. In a competitive labour market, employers and workers interact freely to set wages at a level that maximizes employment opportunities. Across the economy, wages are more likely to be low or rise slowly when there is a large number of unemployed workers. Wages represent a major expense in the production of goods and services. Low wages may encourage firms to hire additional workers to expand production. An increase in hiring reduces the level of unemployment and causes wages to rise. In a competitive labour market, the wage adjustment process ensures greater job opportunities for all workers. When economic conditions are favourable, firms have strong sales prospects and are more willing to pay higher wages in order to attract additional workers. Under unfavourable economic conditions, the revenue prospects of firms decline and they may be forced to cut wages and lay off workers. When unemployment is high, wages are likely to keep falling until they reach levels that make it attractive for firms to start hiring again. When wages are flexible and adjust to economic conditions, employment opportunities are maximized in an economy, because the wage adjustment process creates easier hiring conditions (i.e., low wages) in periods of high unemployment and tougher hiring conditions (high wages) in periods of low unemployment.

In practice, the wage adjustment process can be very slow and painful. Reducing wages and laying off staff can be very challenging. A precondition for having competitive labour markets is that each employer enjoys great flexibility over his decision to hire and fire workers and employees enjoy flexibility over their decision to work and which employer to work for. Another important condition is that no employer or group of employees can have significant influence over the wage setting process. In practice, some countries have strict labour laws that make it very expensive to lay-off staff. Some very large firms and employee unions may be able to influence wages and distort the proper functioning of the labour market. Furthermore, some employers may face a particularly high cost of losing employees with critical skills and may be more willing to pay higher than market wages to retain these critical staff even when business prospects are poor.

In a competitive labour market, the greater availability of employment opportunities increases the mobility of labour. In a competitive labour market, wages are set at an equilibrium level that maximizes employment opportunities for all workers and jobs of comparable skill pay similar wages. In this environment of low unemployment and comparable wages for a given skills category, changing jobs or temporarily entering or leaving the labour market (e.g., for skills training or family reasons) is less costly. Under less competitive conditions, especially when wages are set above the equilibrium level (for welfare or strategic reasons), there may be fewer employment opportunities in the economy.

In a number of developing countries, the government is the main provider of formal employment opportunities and sets wages with a welfare objective. Such countries typically have low levels of employee mobility in the economy, and many workers spend their entire career with the same employer. Such employees are "captured" by higher than normal wages, which in turn creates higher than normal levels of unemployment among workers of comparable skill. In such countries, public sector employees appear to have won a permanent "lottery ticket" and earn wages that command high levels of affordability compared to that of equally qualified peers working in the private sector.

High levels of job creation in an economy support a general increase in wage levels. High levels of job creation in an economy can improve prospects for all employees, because the availability of a larger number of jobs creates greater demand for workers. On the other hand, when the level of employment creation is low and there are too many unemployed people looking for work in every skill category, employees have less bargaining power (they compete too aggressively against themselves), and wages may be generally low. In all countries, employment levels and wages tend to increase during periods of economic expansion because there are more job opportunities. Wages and employment levels tend to fall during an economic contraction. Local employment conditions determine the level of wages in the economy. This includes wages in industries that sell to a global market. For example, mining is a global business, mining products are sold on the global market, and mining equipment is sourced from global suppliers, but miners in countries with low levels of formal employment can earn substantially less than peers in other countries even though their value creation or productivity may be quite similar. For parts of the mining industry where skills may be easily exportable into other countries, wages are more likely to be globally competitive.

In effect, wage levels depend on the productivity and utilization rate of labour (amount of labour required vs. what is available) in an economy or for a skills category. Rising employee productivity in an economy can lead to greater employment opportunities (greater utilization of labour resources) and higher wages.

WHY DO SOME JOBS PAY BETTER THAN OTHERS?
Why do employees with comparable skills sometimes earn substantially different wages?

Skilled jobs require significant investment in training, and need to pay higher wages to encourage people to undertake this investment. When in demand, a number of jobs may pay much higher than average wages because the availability of appropriately skilled people for those jobs may be limited by long training periods, multiple certification requirements, and long work-experience requirements, among others. Such jobs may need to structurally pay higher than average wages in order to encourage people to invest considerable amounts of time, effort, and financial resources in the long and challenging training process to acquire the necessary skills. Because the supply of such specialized skills is limited at any given point, a sudden rise in demand could result in wages rising much faster than average. On the other hand, the large investment in skills training makes such workers more reluctant to seek alternative job opportunities when these skills are not in demand. Due to the poor quality of labour-market information, a considerable number of people may undertake these long investments based on a perception of the "importance" of a skill for the economy rather than accurate information about realistic employment opportunities for that skill.

Employees who work for more productive and financially successful firms may earn higher wages than peers with comparable skills who work for less financially successful firms. In a competitive market, a productive employee who generates greater economic value for his employer deserves to be paid higher wages, or he may leave to work for a competitor or start his own business (if this is feasible). In practice, most jobs involve working in teams, and it may be very difficult to quantify the economic value created by an individual employee. It may be more feasible to measure the economic value created by a team, a business unit, or an entire firm. As a result, employees in more productive and financially successful firms may earn higher wages than peers with comparable skills that work in less financially successful firms.

In 1914, Henry Ford, the founder of the Ford Motor Company, doubled assembly-line employee wages to five dollars a day (this was double the existing market wage at the time). Following the announcement of the wage increase, long queues of workers lined up for an opportunity to work at Ford. Ford's assembly-line innovation improved worker productivity and made it possible for Ford to pay higher wages in order to attract more reliable workers. The nature of assembly-line production meant that, lower levels of absenteeism and employee turnover had a material impact on productivity. With more reliable workers, Ford could produce many more cars per day at a much lower cost. Ford himself described the wage increase to five dollars a day as "one of the finest cost cutting moves we ever made." Between 1914 and 1916, profits doubled at Ford Motor, supported by higher employee productivity. Ford could afford to pay much higher wages than the market because it had a technology advantage (the assembly line) that could deliver greater economic value for the company with a more reliable work force.

Employees whose productivity initiatives can be measured directly are more likely to earn higher wages. An employee whose productivity or economic value creation can be objectively and directly measured has the potential to earn higher than average wages within a firm. When firms are unable to distinguish between productive and unproductive employees and therefore pay a comparable wage to both, they are effectively subsidizing the unproductive workers at the expense of the good ones. Productive workers may be less reactive to this observation because their productivity may be partly dependent on that of their colleagues, and it may be difficult to convince other employers of their superior productivity.

Skills that allow for granular assessment of productivity at the individual employee level can enable productive employees to earn higher than average wages. For example, successful salespeople in pharmaceutical companies may earn more than the scientists doing research because the economic value created by the salesperson can be assessed more objectively. It is possible to know exactly how much economic value (in sales and profits) that a salesperson creates for a firm over a given period. Because of such high levels of visibility into economic value creation, firms are better able to link the compensation of individual salespeople to their productivity. Furthermore, because the value created is transparent and objective, when the employee does not receive adequate compensation for his efforts, he is in a stronger position to transfer his skills to competing employers. Their hiring decision, in turn, becomes much easier because the potential value-add is more obvious.

An employer may pay higher than market wages to retain critical staff whose value to the firm may exceed that which could be obtained by hiring new workers with comparable skills. Critical roles and highly skilled positions that are difficult or costly to replace tend to pay higher than market wages in order to provide key employees with greater incentives to stay with their current employer. Some firms face a high cost of losing key employees who may have knowledge about trade secrets or critical production processes. The loss of such critical staff could result in a reduction in productivity levels or a loss of competitiveness. For example, in innovative engineering companies, engineers who have worked on key projects and acquired critical know-how in the process are of greater value to a firm than engineers with comparable skills who work outside the firm. The loss of a key engineer may lead to a disruption in a firm's ability to produce certain products or services. A competing firm may also be interested in paying higher than market wages to attract such employees for the critical knowledge they have developed on the job.

Some specialist roles involve working in teams and fitting into a firm's "culture" and may take a long time to fill. For such roles, firms may be willing to pay higher than market wages to increase their chances of finding the "right" person for the job and to help retain critical staff. For example, the requirements for hiring a business director in a company go beyond practical skills and include several intangible factors that may affect the director's ability to effectively work within a team to obtain the best results. Even when there are many adequately qualified people for the role, most companies spend a significant amount of time and resources to find the "right fit." A wrong choice may be costly to the firm. It may weaken team morale, lower productivity levels, cause a loss of other key staff or customers, and may depress levels of profitability.

On the other hand, wages associated with low-skilled jobs or positions that can easily be filled tend to be low and representative of market wages. These roles or skills typically require little training. The loss of a low skilled employee has a limited impact on overall value creation in a company. Such jobs, even when they are in a highly profitable company, tend to pay low market wages because they can be refilled time and again without subjecting the firm to significant risks. The large supply of potential workers for such roles keeps the market wage at low levels. For example, supermarket operators pay low market wages (often close to the minimum wage set by law) because they employ workers who can be easily replaced with a negligible impact on sales. They can provide the training needed to do the job over a short period. Positions are easy to fill, and the supermarket's ability to create value is not negatively affected by a high employee turnover rate. Supermarkets can comfortably cope with losing and replacing up to half of their employees every year. For other retailers, such as clothing or electronics shops, higher levels of employee knowledge and customer service translate into higher sales and profits. The loss of well-trained employees has a greater impact on sales, and such retailers spend more resources in training and compensating employees when compared to food retailers.

Work Experience. In most organizations wage levels tend to increase with the number of years of work experience. In a number of cases, this observation can be economically justified because experience can increase the productivity of workers. By focusing on the development of key skills and processes on the job, workers can improve the levels of their skills and get better at the job. Experience also prepares people to take on greater responsibility in an organization.

However, numerous institutions generally follow a tradition of aligning wage increases with work experience without seeking evidence of employee productivity gains to justify such increases. For example, while a few years of experience increases the productivity of teachers (i.e., their ability to improve student knowledge), there is no strong evidence to suggest that teachers who have been in the classroom for decades are more productive than young teachers with three to five years of experience. Some teachers may develop great teaching techniques with long years of experience. For others, years of experience may reduce their level of enthusiasm for the profession. In some institutions, employees may automatically come up for promotion in rank and salary once certain levels of experience are attained, even when there have been no changes in productivity levels or work requirements. Because individual employee productivity may be difficult to measure, all employers implicitly use experience as a proxy for productivity to varying degrees.

Changes in Industry Conditions. Sometimes the security of employment and wage prospects may be affected more by changes in industry conditions than the productivity initiatives of firms and their employees. For example, the employment and wage prospects of workers employed in mining, and firms that supply equipment and services to the mining industry can significantly be impacted by changes in commodity prices. Employees and capital providers in a poorly managed and inefficient mining firm may earn lower levels of financial compensation compared to those associated with a highly productive mining firm. However, falling commodity prices is an industry phenomenon and bodes poorly for jobs, wages, and profits of all firms and stakeholders that derive earnings from the mining industry.

Some employers with large financial resources may have an explicit welfare goal and pay higher than normal wages. In a truly competitive market, firms make normal profits that provide adequate (or fair) compensation for the capital, labour, and other resources employed in production. In a competitive market for goods, firms do not have the power to influence prices in order to substantially increase their profits, and no employer can sustain paying wages that exceed the productivity levels of their employees. Through competitive interaction between workers and employers, wages are set at "normal" or equilibrium levels that maximize employment opportunities. However, in practice, the level of competition in some industries may be low, and some firms may have the power to influence prices and earn higher than normal levels of profitability. For example, through government regulation or a technology advantage, a firm could be the primary supplier of a product. This strong position can provide the firm with the power to raise prices and earn supernormal profits. Supported by their extraordinary profitability, the owners and managers of such companies can afford to pay higher than normal wages to their employees (if they choose to). In general, employees have a strong preference for firms with dominant market positions and strong brands. Firms with strong market positions may have greater financial resources to pay attractive salaries and provide superior working conditions.

In a number of countries, the government is one of the largest providers of formal jobs and may use its extensive financial resources and tax collecting ability to pay higher than market wages with a primary goal of promoting employee welfare. Firms may sometimes raise wage levels above the "normal or market" rate to attract more reliable employees. Paying higher than market wages may have a negative impact on job creation when a large employer is involved. When companies that have the ability and willingness to pay higher than market wages are large employers in an industry, their actions can raise wage expectations for the whole industry. By raising the cost of labour for all other businesses in the industry, their actions may reduce employment opportunities.

Competition among firms and among employees seeking the most rewarding job opportunities supports innovation and productivity. The ability of large market-dominating employers to attract the most talented and reliable workers by paying high welfare wages may stifle productivity and innovation in the rest of the economy. In a competitive market, higher profits are linked to firms that produce the most desirable products at the most competitive prices, and there is a stronger link between wages and employee productivity. This merit-based system of compensation creates strong incentives for firms and employees to innovate and be productive. Highly successful firms may pay higher than normal wages to attract the best talent, but when these firms are large enough to influence the market wage for skills, they can create indirect but strong headwinds to innovation and employment growth in the rest of the economy.

FACTORS THAT CONTRIBUTE TO DISTORTING THE PROPER FUNCTIONING OF LABOUR MARKETS CAN RAISE THE LEVEL OF UNEMPLOYMENT IN THE ECONOMY.

Poor quality information about employment opportunities, wages levels, and working conditions in the economy. Poor job market information increases the costs involved in matching employee skills to available job opportunities and can increase the level of unemployment. Government employment programs that provide information about the availability of jobs and basic job training can help to resolve this problem for low skilled jobs and situations in which firms are least sensitive about sharing employment and wage information.

Rigidities in the mobility and adaptability of labour to new employment opportunities. Even when the economy is creating new job opportunities, there may be high levels of unemployment when these new opportunities require people to relocate or retrain to acquire new skills. A spouse may choose to endure long periods of unemployment with the hope of finding a job in the locality of the present household when there could be job opportunities available in a distant location. It may also be challenging to re-train low skilled workers to take up highly skilled positions that require several years of intense training.

Unemployment benefits. Generous unemployment benefits may promote higher levels of unemployment; people receiving income support may be less interested in seeking employment or may be more selective in taking up available job opportunities. Such income-support measures can exaggerate the true level of unemployment (i.e., the number of people *actively* looking for work). Unemployment benefits are typically paid for a limited period (about a year) to lessen their negative impact.

Minimum-wage laws set by the government. Minimum-wage laws are set by the government as a welfare initiative to ensure a minimum level of affordability for all workers. However, some activities generate low economic value and may not be viable at the legal minimum wage. Even in countries where minimum wage laws are better enforced, there are instances where small businesses may (illegally) offer to pay workers below the minimum wage, and employees may accept this offer when it is their only viable source of employment and income. The free interaction of workers and employers sets wages at levels that maximize job opportunities for all workers. When the minimum wage is set above the equilibrium wage that maximizes job opportunities in the economy, unemployment rates can rise even as people with jobs enjoy higher levels of affordability. Progressive governments will typically set the minimum wage at a level that ensures that the greater majority of firms can afford to pay it. In this way, minimum-wage laws can protect the welfare of workers without inhibiting job creation.

Union power. By binding their interests together to negotiate as one party, union workers improve their bargaining position against employers and typically earn higher wages compared to nonunionized workers in similar roles. Unionization may arise from a desperate attempt by workers to increase their bargaining power in an effort to earn wages that adequately cover basic living expenses. Unions may also be formed to help workers bargain for a greater share of the economic value they help to create within a firm or an industry. Unions are more likely to occur in industries dominated by a small number of large employers. Large employers that have excessive influence in setting wages may sometimes use this influence to depress wages below levels that could be justified by employee productivity. In some cases, unions may be necessary to counterbalance the power of an overly influential employer, particularly in an environment of high unemployment, low mobility of labour in a particular region (e.g., employees of a mining company on an island or remote part of a country), and low transferability of employee skills (e.g., a nuclear engineer may have limited employment options outside the nuclear industry, which is typically controlled by a few large firms or the government). Through their stronger bargaining position, the higher wages that unions earn for their members may increase the costs of doing business and hinder the ability of companies to expand. The propensity of unions to support higher wages over employment opportunities is most obvious under poor economic conditions when unions typically vote in favour of maintaining or raising their wage levels at the expense of some members being laid off. The alternative scenario of full employment for all members at the expense of lower wage increases or modest wage cuts hardly ever wins the vote.

Above market wages paid by a large influential employer. Competition in the labour market can be distorted by a large influential employer. When a large influential employer is willing and able to pay higher than market wages, this may increase the cost of hiring for all other businesses and may reduce employment levels in an economy.

5

JOB CREATION

Imagination is one of humanity's greatest qualities-without it, there would be no innovation, advancement or technology, and the world will be a very dull place.
-—Richard Branson, founder of the Virgin Group.

Jobs provide a critical lifeline to people in every society. Within the set of conditions necessary for maintaining adequate living standards, governments and other highly influential institutions appear to have the least control over job creation. Job creation is a challenge even for powerful governments who have won great battles, undertaken monumental infrastructure projects, and (in some cases) managed to send missions to distant planets.

Individuals, firms, and institutions that create jobs are the true heroes of any economy. Their efforts help to solve a major societal problem for which there is no clear and guaranteed solution. Education institutions have succeeded in training people as doctors, teachers, engineers, and providers of other essential services that people require to improve their well-being. For example, for our healthcare needs, medical schools have been so successful in training doctors that they can implicitly "guarantee" an adequate level of performance for each graduate. However, when it comes to job creation, governments and educational institutions have been far less successful in training people to deliver one of the most essential requirements of life. The task of job creation is enormous and requires the support of the whole society. An economy that manages to create high levels of employment is likely to produce more and support higher living standards than a comparable economy that is not able to fully utilize its labour resources.

POLICIES THAT PROMOTE THE PURSUIT OF INITIATIVES THAT HAVE THE POTENTIAL TO CREATE ECONOMIC VALUE OFFER AN AVENUE FOR JOB CREATION

Jobs are created as a consequence of initiatives that generate economic value. Therefore, regulation and policies that promote innovation and entrepreneurial activities can support higher levels of job creation. Entrepreneurial firms and individuals direct their efforts into creating new products and services or improving upon existing products to make them more desirable.

The entrepreneurial process is challenging and requires a significant commitment of resources into initiatives that inherently have slim chances of becoming successful. Firms may channel financial resources into research and development projects which may not deliver their intended results. The development of a new product or service often requires significant investment, but sales prospects of the product may remain highly uncertain. A firm with a successful line of products may make reasonable assumptions about growth opportunities and invest in expansion. While the uncertainty associated with expanding the production capacity for an existing product may be lower than introducing new product, there is no guarantee that these efforts will succeed long enough to pay back the capital invested in the expansion. If entrepreneurial efforts at starting new businesses and expanding existing ones were inherently more successful, unemployment will not be a major challenge.

Apple founder, Steve Jobs, had this to say about entrepreneurial challenges:
I'm convinced that about half of what separates the successful entrepreneurs from the non-successful ones is pure perseverance. It is so hard. You put so much of your life into this thing. There are such rough moments in time that I think most people give up. I don't blame them. It's really tough and it consumes your life. If you've got a family and you're in the early days of a company, I can't imagine how one could do it. I'm sure it's been done, but it's rough. It's pretty much an eighteen hour day job, seven days a week for a while. Unless you have a lot of passion about this, you're not going to survive. You're going to give it up. So you've got to have an idea, or a problem or a wrong that you want to right that you're passionate about otherwise you're not going to have the perseverance to stick it through. I think that's half the battle right there.

Notwithstanding the magnitude of the challenge, it is still essential for a society to support entrepreneurial efforts in a responsible way. This is because one successful outcome has the potential to create immense value for society through the development of products and services that can improve lives, increase productivity, and serve as a platform for job creation with ripple effects throughout the economy. Societies that promote an innovative and entrepreneurial culture may be more successful in creating jobs in the long term. A large number of products that improve our productivity and quality of life such as the electric bulb, dishwashers, cars, computers and smartphones, were all at one point, a big gamble for entrepreneurial firms and individuals.

The trial-and-error process of entrepreneurial initiatives is a necessary precondition for sustainable economic growth and job creation. Businesses spend significant amounts of capital on research and development that may not produce intended results on many occasions. However, without this effort, the rate of innovation and improvement in living standards would be limited. When successful, firms that invest in innovation typically enjoy the fastest rate of growth and help to expand opportunities for creating jobs in the economy. In the early part of the twentieth century, Ford Motor Company was one of the most innovative firms and one of the fastest growing companies in the world. Supported by Ford's assembly-line technology innovation, the growth of the auto industry created ripple effects that generated employment in several other sectors of the economy. Today, firms like Google, Apple, and Facebook are leaders in innovation and have been enjoying superior revenue growth. Their innovations have the potential to accelerate the pace of job creation in the economy. In a similar manner, countries that invest a greater share of their national income in research and development and other entrepreneurial initiatives are likely to enjoy a higher rate of economic growth in relation to their peers.

The General Electric (GE) equation illustrates how a commitment to innovation and entrepreneurial initiatives can support human progress while creating attractive returns for all stakeholders (including employees, customers, shareholders, and governments). By focusing on innovation and value creation for its customers, General Electric has evolved from its early foundations, built on the invention of the electric light bulb (by Thomas Edison in 1872), to maintain its relevance in providing industrial and technology solutions in present times. Today, GE is a market leader in building jet engines, power generation equipment, healthcare equipment and household appliances for the global market, and employs over three hundred thousand people in its global operations.

Figure 5.1.

The General Electric (GE) Equation

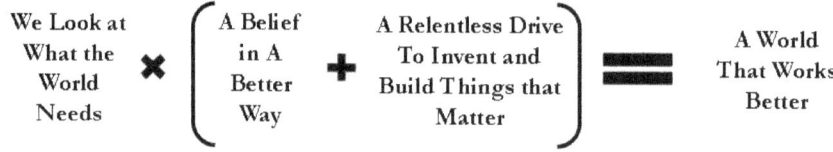

Source: GE

Imagination is critical for step changes in value creation. This is what Richard Branson, founder of the Virgin Group, had to say on the subject:
Imagination is one of humanity's greatest qualities – without it, there would be no innovation, advancement or technology, and the world would be a very dull place. I was recently asked to sum up what I do in just five words, to which I answered: I like to create things. Creativity is a direct offshoot of imagination, and is essential not only to life, but to business too. Creativity and imagination are driving forces behind most things

we do, and have been the key to many of our successes.

The business world often gets caught up in facts and figures, and forgets the importance of imagination and creativity. Like Albert Einstein said: "The intuitive mind is a sacred gift, and the rational mind is a faithful servant. We have created a society that honours the servant and has forgotten the gift." While the details and data are important in business, the ability to dream, conceptualize and invent is what sets the successful and the unsuccessful apart – and in life, often the happy from the unhappy.

Imagination should be intertwined in daily life, and not just restricted to problem solving. Imagination gives hope, drive and inspiration, and is incredibly motivational. In that sense, dreaming should not be the reward, but instead a habit. The fruits that come from the success of achieving a dream should be the reward. It is a natural human instinct to want to know what lies before us. By dreaming and imagining, we can effectively chart our own paths, and see what we already believe to be true. Don't limit yourself to what you know and what you have been told to be true. If you use your imagination you will be presented with opportunities and possibilities beyond your wildest dreams.

MEASURES THAT CAN STIMULATE THE DEVELOPMENT OF ENTREPRENEURIAL INITIATIVES

Individuals and firms pursuing entrepreneurial initiatives rely on the availability of key resources, such as appropriately skilled employees, like-minded resource networks, and funding to help them pursue their dreams. Initiatives that lower the cost of these resources and eliminate other barriers to the entrepreneurial process may help increase entrepreneurial activity and improve chances of success.

Cultural appreciation of the invaluable role entrepreneurs play in society is an important first step in encouraging entrepreneurial activity. Entrepreneurs often make deliberate but tough decisions to forgo desirable opportunities in order to concentrate on ideas that they are most passionate about. They trade predictable and sometimes well-paying job opportunities for a life of long, hard working hours and great economic uncertainty. Businesses that make bold decisions to invest in innovation or develop new products and services often risk a substantial amount of capital, employee resources, and management credibility in pursuing these initiatives.

Successful entrepreneurs and business leaders ought to be local or national heroes because they take on immense challenges and help solve the number one economic problem for most people. The potential value they create for society is priceless. Unlike most jobs, where effective training can guarantee a decent performance, a successful entrepreneur is a truly extraordinary achiever.

A society that is supportive of entrepreneurial initiatives would also appreciate people associated with unsuccessful entrepreneurial efforts. This is because the entrepreneurial process, even when it is unsuccessful, helps to build a wealth of invaluable skills such as creativity, perseverance, team spirit, and critical and original thinking. These skills are valuable in all other economic activities. Education institutions can support the creation of an entrepreneurial culture by promoting greater creativity, critical thinking, and entrepreneurial initiatives in school. An entrepreneur-friendly culture is more likely to grow in countries with a larger number of visible entrepreneur-led success stories. While the chances of success may be collectively low, the visible impact of a few high-profile successful initiatives can have an enduring stimulatory effect.

The establishment of entrepreneurial and business communities where people can share ideas and inspire each other can stimulate entrepreneurial initiatives. Entrepreneurs often have atypical personalities that embody high levels of motivation, creativity, originality in thought, perseverance, and the courage to pursue an unconventional path that has the potential to create enormous value for society. Entrepreneurial business leaders can often be lonely voices within their own organizations when they undertake investments in new and often higher risk products. Formal and informal support networks for these heroes of society, who put themselves on the line and take bold steps that most people would shy away from, could be instrumental in stimulating entrepreneurial initiatives.

The development of appropriate funding opportunities. To ensure sustainability, entrepreneurial and innovative initiatives need suitable funding structures that can accommodate the high-risk characteristics associated with such ventures. Financing for unproven but high-potential innovative products and services can be a major challenge even for established companies with a recognized track record. The availability of an appropriate funding mechanism can expand the scope of entrepreneurial activities and potentially improve the chances of success. The appropriate funding mechanism must be able to diversify risk across a number of potentially exciting opportunities and absorb complete losses in individual cases.

In some countries, there are well-developed, dedicated funding structures for entrepreneurs, such as venture-capital funds and platforms that pool the resources of groups of high income individual investors (angel investors). The contribution of venture capital and angel investors goes beyond providing funds in exchange for a share of the economic value of an entrepreneurial project. Venture capital and angel investors may also create stronger incentives for entrepreneurs to execute on their dreams, provide oversight and feedback on entrepreneurial development, and can inject additional expertise and other resources to improve the chances of success. The growth of the venture-capital industry and other entrepreneur friendly finance structures has been supported by the high financial rewards, excitement, and transformational human experience that have been observed in a number of successful entrepreneurial initiatives in some countries. The availability of professionally managed funding structures makes it possible to invest in a portfolio of different entrepreneurial initiatives to diversify the inherent risk associated with each investment. Risk is further diversified by capital providers who typically allocate fractional shares of their capital into such funds.

The risk characteristics and appropriate funding structure for an entrepreneurial activity change through its stages of development. An entrepreneur will typically start a business venture with his or her own resources and those of immediate family and friends. At the early stage, his willingness to work long hours for little or no money (sweat equity) may be a meaningful component of his capital. Gaining access to external funding can be challenging, and is more likely to occur at later stages of product/idea development. In certain countries, the funding industry is so well developed that some venture capital investors will typically concentrate on investing in projects in a particular stage of development and find other capital providers to take on funding for later stages. The availability of funds that focus on specific stages of business development generates more detailed understanding of the risk characteristics associated with each stage, and supports the development of expertise in dealing with stage specific challenges.

The development of crowdfunding platforms in recent years has been a major boost to entrepreneurship, innovation, and creativity. Crowdfunding platforms provide opportunities for individuals around the world to support innovative and entrepreneurial initiatives. These platforms provide an efficient way for entrepreneurs to gain financial support from thousands of potential investors over the Internet. Crowdfunding also provides an accessible opportunity for high income savers to buy shares in early stage businesses. The scope of crowdfunded initiatives is wide-ranging. School children have raised hundreds of dollars to fund creative projects, and some young entrepreneurs have raised millions of dollars for their projects through this accessible platform.

Well-developed financial markets can stimulate entrepreneurial initiatives within existing businesses. In well-developed financial markets, financial intermediaries such as banks and dedicated investment firms have strong incentives to independently analyze investment prospects and allocate capital to firms with the most promising opportunities. Their strong incentive to represent the interest of capital providers, increases the willingness of savers to provide funds and lowers the cost of capital for all businesses in the economy. Greater availability of funding at a lower cost stimulates entrepreneurial initiatives and improves the job creation potential.

A well-developed capital market increases the amount of capital resources available for different types of investment and creates greater efficiency in allocating capital to firms with the most promising prospects. Well-developed capital markets increase the diversity of capital providers and make it possible to fund a wider range of capital needs. Some investors may be more capable of taking on higher investment risk in exchange for greater long-term financial rewards. Such investors are more likely to allocate a portion of their savings to companies that are investing in innovative products with attractive long-term revenue growth potential. On the other hand, capital providers such as people on retirement, may rely on their investments for regular income and may have less appetite for high-risk investments.

Ultimately, the ability to come up with entrepreneur or investment friendly funding structures depends on savings habits in a given country and whether it has developed a culture that proactively supports entrepreneurial activity. A history of some high impact entrepreneur success stories can create greater cultural acceptance for financing such activities. A few success stories can make a much deeper impression than many failures.

For example, many technology firms around the world find it more attractive to raise capital in the United States, where there has been a longer history of technology success stories and a deeper level of investor experience in providing capital to technology firms than in other countries. A growing entrepreneurial culture can be self-reinforcing. Countries that have experienced a large number of successful entrepreneurial initiatives tend to have many financially successful entrepreneurs and investors who are more likely to take greater interest in supporting young entrepreneurs. This virtuous cycle can inspire an entrepreneurial drive across generations.

Incentives that reward productivity and innovation can stimulate economic-value creation and employment growth. In many cases, the real genius in innovation and entrepreneurial success is found in execution rather than idea generation. In the challenging and highly uncertain path of attempting to launch new products and services, success is often anchored on a few key individuals whose motivation, creativity, tireless effort, and passion resuscitate projects from several near-death encounters until they are finally well executed and successful. People who start businesses are often highly motivated and have strong incentives to execute. However, to be successful, individuals and businesses pursuing entrepreneurial initiatives need to create strong incentives for other key people on their teams. Employees are more likely to execute better if they have strong incentives that reward superior effort and productivity. Employees are more likely to put more effort into their work and take greater ownership of results if their financial compensation and opportunities for promotion are linked to results at both the individual and team levels. Incentive systems that link rewards to productivity and help inspire economic ownership mentality among employees can stimulate higher value creation and ultimately support a greater number of vibrant economic activities.

WHO ARE THE BENEFICIARIES OF INNOVATION AND ENTREPRENEURIAL SUCCESS?

Case Study 5.1: The Impact of Apple's iPhone and iPad Innovations

The global consumer benefits. Apple released the first iPhone in 2007 and the iPad in 2010. These products created so much value for consumers that they were willing to pay higher prices for them (cheaper alternatives had inferior functionality). The iPhone started the smartphone revolution by capitalizing on advances in computer technology to produce a user friendly mobile phone that was also a powerful minicomputer. With the touch of a finger, iPhone users could access the Internet, store data, access media and entertainment, and take high resolution pictures and movies (a feature that rendered standalone digital cameras increasingly redundant). Apple's smartphone innovation enabled the development of mobile-phone software applications (apps) that allow for more user friendly ways to use the Internet. By allowing direct entry into key Internet sites or functions with the push of a button, apps have created a step change in productivity for mobile phone users. Consumers are now spending more time on their smartphones, and talking on the phone is no longer the primary function.

Supported by the wide global consumer adoption of these new products, in 2013, Apple generated sales of $170 billion compared to sales of $19 billion in 2007. In 2013 alone, Apple sold over 150 million iPhones (contributing about $90 billion in revenue) and 70 million iPads (contributing $30 billion in revenue for that year). Globalization allows the best products to reach every corner of the world in record time, and Apple was able to generate over 60 percent of its sales outside of North America in 2013, with Europe, Japan, and China being major contributors to this sales growth. The overall sales attributable to the iPhone and iPad provide a useful estimate of the value consumers are deriving from this innovation.

Remarkable surge in Apple shareholder returns. With profits growing from $2 billion in 2006 (the year before the iPhone was launched) to $37 billion in 2013, clearly the owners (i.e., the shareholders) of Apple made tremendous gains on their investment in the company. From January 2007 to December 2013, the value of the company (whose shares are actively traded in the stock market) rose over six fold to $500 billion from $80 billion and made Apple not only the most valuable company in the United States, but the most valuable company in the world.

Who are the Apple shareholders or owners who added over $400 billion to their wealth over these years? The great attraction of well-developed stock markets is their ability to draw capital from a large number of people. This allows for the spreading of risks as well as the sharing of rewards associated with investing in innovation. The great majority of Apple shares is owned by the general public. On the Apple shareholder register, the key holders are financial intermediaries and professional investors who primarily invest pension contributions and other savings on behalf of millions of individuals, companies, and some local governments. There is also a large number of individual investors who respond to their enthusiasm for Apple products by buying shares directly. Because of globalization of capital markets, the opportunity to own bits of Apple (the biggest bite one can manage on this rather big apple) is not restricted to pensioners and individual savers in the United States; it is equally open to savers and professional investors from the rest of the world.

Apple employees have benefited from the company's success in a number of ways. Rising sales and rising profits at Apple supported employment growth and increases in employee compensation. Apple's full-time employees worldwide increased from eighteen thousand people in 2006 to over eighty thousand people by 2013. The exponential growth of Apple sales and profits and, perhaps more importantly, the exponential growth in industries that emerged from Apple's innovation created rising demand for specialized skills in software engineering and app development and higher wages for employees with those skills.

As part of its compensation policy and efforts to retain talent, Apple rewards employees and management with stock options that make it possible for employees to benefit from an increase in the value of the company. Apple also offers all employees the option of buying up to $25,000 a year in Apple shares at a 15 percent discount. Supported by the considerable increase in the value of the company, Apple employees who took up this option and contributed the maximum $25,000 every year between 2007 and 2013 ended up with about $1 million by the end of the period.

Significant job creation in the United States and the global economy: the multiplier effect of innovation. Apple commissioned an independent study that revealed that even though the company employed only fifty-thousand full-time employees in the United States, Apple's innovation supported the creation of over six-hundred thousand jobs in the United States by 2012. About half of the total jobs created, came through the "app economy" that Apple's innovation made possible. Within six years of the iPhone innovation, over one million apps had been developed with more than 50 billion app downloads. This generated tens of billions of dollars in revenue for app developers around the world.

Apple's innovation has created a far greater number of jobs in the global economy. The manufacturing and assembly of Apple products in Asia, the app economy that is developing rapidly all over the world and retail opportunities from selling Apple products and other smartphones are likely to have created far more jobs outside the United States. For example, in 2014, Apple estimated that the app economy it helped pioneer, had created over five-hundred thousand jobs in Europe. Apple's innovation has also opened up opportunities for technology companies around the world to sell into a much larger market for mobile phones. This is a great example of how globalization helps to create value and jobs across the world irrespective of the source of innovation.

A broad number of other beneficiaries: In 2013, Apple paid $13 billion in taxes to governments around the world on the profits of its operations. Apple has increased its spending on research and development to support future product development initiatives. The step change in consumer experience and Internet accessibility that the iPhone inspired has stimulated the growth of a large number of industries such as online advertising, social networking, and e-commerce, where a large number of jobs are being created.

*****

The Role of the Progressive Employee in Job Creation

It is far easier and much safer to invest in higher education or skills training and assume an employee role than to create jobs. A typical employee shows up to work, does what is expected of him, gets paid, and walks out of the door without much consideration of the competitive risks or growth opportunities that his employer may be presented with. Such passive employee behavior may not promote productivity and is less supportive of business growth and job creation.

The role of a progressive employee is essential in improving the prospects of existing businesses. Progressive employees take interest in their jobs, understand how their employers create economic value (i.e., how revenue and profits are earned), understand their role in the value-creating process, and help to make themselves and their employers relevant by being proactive in executing responsibilities and coming up with creative ideas to improve business processes. Progressive employees contribute towards the growth and sustainability of business and support the creation of more jobs in the process. Progressive firms understand the immense value creating potential embedded in dedicated employees, and they spend considerable resources to motivate and develop employee skills for the benefit of their aligned interests. Improvements in productivity usually mean higher revenue and profit growth, greater opportunities for promotion, and higher wages for employees. Within the same industry, it is not surprising that employees of financially successful firms tend to earn more than their peers who work for less productive firms.

Every individual is an important stakeholder in the job-creation process and has influence over the eventual long-term outcome through his savings (or consumption) habits, which has an impact on the amount and cost of capital available in the economy, his education and skills-development efforts, and his interest in supporting productivity initiations of his employer. Individuals have to assume some responsibility for creating value. The potential for entrepreneurship and self-improvement lies within everyone. At the very basic level, businesses are started to provide solutions to very practical needs. Everyone can think of a new product or better approach to doing something that increases convenience or desirability, and therefore, has the potential to be an entrepreneur within his or her current employment and in other aspects of daily life.

Promoting Creativity and Entrepreneurship in Youth. A large number of businesses were started by individuals who found commercially viable ways to pursue their interests. A number of high-profile technology companies (Microsoft, Google, Apple, and Facebook) were started by young individuals who opted out of potentially attractive career options to follow their interests in developing technology that had the potential to transform the way we do things. An education and a culture that promote creativity and entrepreneurship among young people could be a powerful investment in long-term job creation.

Youth offers a precious moment for fueling entrepreneurial initiatives. Students and young adults, have a unique opportunity to channel their energy into pursuing their interests. Young people have an immense capacity to imagine new possibilities. The costs associated with pursuing one's interest may be lower in youth than later in life, when one is likely to be burdened with greater financial responsibility (for oneself and family). Freedom from financial responsibilities and routine employment schedules can support higher levels of creativity in youth. When successful, young entrepreneurs can be a beacon of hope for a whole generation and can stimulate creativity in many sectors of the economy. There is no major downside to pursuing one's interests; the process is enriching by itself. It enables the development of strong skills that help to enhance one's potential in other areas. A progressive employer is more likely to admire a young candidate who, in addition to being well educated, has pursued an entrepreneurial initiative or an individual interest to an advanced level than a competing candidate with a similar education background but with limited interests and experiences.

THE ROLE OF GOVERNMENTS IN JOB CREATION

The government has powerful influence over the development of job-creation opportunities in any country. Through its regulatory powers and mandate to provide public infrastructure and social services, the government can lower hurdles for job creators. In executing its role in providing administrative and social services, the government directly creates a considerable number of jobs. It has the potential to support the creation of many more jobs by enacting policies and upholding practices that support the ambitions of citizens and businesses to invest and innovate. Policies that support economic stability, stability in the value of money or prices, low interest rates, low and predictable tax rates, flexible labour laws, education and research, have the potential to support job creation.

Education. Businesses require human resources to function and employee costs are one of the highest cost items for most industries. When skills are in short supply, high employee costs can restrict the growth rates of businesses and new start-ups. The government is a major investor in education in most countries and can help lower the cost of skilled labour. Governments can also put in place initiatives to make education relevant to the labour market and help improve the competitiveness of businesses.

Government regulation can either stimulate or stifle growth initiatives of private businesses. Laws that uphold and protect property rights and promote competition can support growth in investment and job creation. High levels of government bureaucracy and regulatory requirements take time and financial resources away from productive work, and they can stifle entrepreneurial initiatives. Labour market regulations can have a material impact on the cost of hiring workers. Inflexible labour laws make it highly costly to lay off staff even when business prospects are declining. When the cost associated with laying off staff is too high, businesses become more reluctant to hire additional workers or will require a high level of certainty in prospects before hiring. Without flexibility in labour market laws, businesses will not be able to maximize opportunities for growth, and the overall number of jobs created will be lower than it could otherwise have been. Inflexible labour laws may pressure a firm with declining prospects to keep more people in employment than required. By bowing to such pressure, a firm could destroy capital that could be channeled into more productive parts of the economy, where sustainable jobs are more likely to be created.

Economic policy. Poor government economic policies can create uncertainty and cripple many entrepreneurial initiatives. Poor economic policies can lead to high inflation, an unstable environment for prices, high interest rates, and adverse prospects for tax rates. In times of great economic uncertainty, there may be less appetite for taking risk, which means that entrepreneurial initiatives may struggle to access funding or attract top talent.

The enormity of a government's financial resources and legal powers may sometimes stifle the development of private enterprise when the government becomes directly involved in the provision of key services that could be adequately supplied by the private sector. Because of its large financial resources and strong legal powers, it is difficult for the government to be a fair competitor in many industries. Government policy should be focused on promoting competition, which stimulates innovation and economic growth.

The majority of jobs in any economy is created by private individuals and businesses, not the government. In some countries, governments play a more significant role in the economy and may be the main provider of formal employment opportunities. However, even in such countries, the private sector remains the dominant provider of jobs in the overall economy. Private-sector entrepreneurial zeal and ability to innovate are key instruments for sustainable job creation. To maximize employment opportunities in the economy, government policies need to be directed at creating a favorable environment for stimulating the economic initiatives of individuals and businesses.

6

THE ECONOMIC RELATIONSHIP BETWEEN CITIZENS AND THEIR GOVERNMENT

The most important political office is that of the private citizen.
—Louis Brandeis (1856–1941), American lawyer and Supreme Court judge.

Governments provide a necessary and efficient mechanism for promoting the welfare of citizens. Imagine a country with no government to administer public services, no police, no traffic rules, no security, no law, no regulation on products and services, no protection for personal property or lives, and no courts to turn to for justice. The result would be an undesirable mess for everyone. Governments play an important administrative and regulatory role for society and have a strong advantage in providing certain key services that are either impossible or too costly for individuals to provide for themselves.

The government has a strong advantage in providing public services such as the police service, the judicial service, and the provision of regulatory oversight in many sectors of the economy. These services are likely to suffer in quality when provided by individuals or businesses. Economic activities of private citizens are directed by a profit seeking motive, an incentive that can destroy the quality and desirability of essential public services that need to maintain fairness and impartiality in securing public welfare. Other important services such as national security and the provision of public roads are highly desirable but unlikely to attract private investment. These services require a large financial investment and are costly to maintain. After the service has been installed, it may be challenging to get individual users or beneficiaries of the service to pay for it. These investments may be essential in promoting public welfare; however, because citizens can effectively free-ride (i.e., enjoy the benefit of a service without paying for it), they are not attractive investments for private businesses. People living in countries with poor infrastructure and inadequate public services often have to pay highly punitive costs for basic security, enforcement of property rights, and access to reliable education, health services, and power supply, often with suboptimal results.

Delivery of public services often relies on private citizens and businesses. A deep and efficient private sector with a strong track record of efficient execution across industries and nimbleness in adapting to changing economic conditions can be supportive to government efforts to deliver services. For example, in several countries, the private sector has taken over the delivery of utility services such as water and electricity supply and telecommunication services from the government. In many cases, private ownership and the competition that it embodies have delivered higher service quality to a greater proportion of citizens, often at a lower cost.

Government policies that promote sustainable economic growth can improve the welfare of citizens. Prudent economic policies can support sustainable economic growth, improve employment opportunities and living standards and support greater political stability. Social upheaval, civil wars, high levels of crime, and lawlessness are far more common in countries where poor polices regularly lead to economic instability. The level of productivity in an economy has a considerable impact on the ability of the government to provide and maintain essential public services. Sustainable economic growth has to be led by the private sector. This is because the government is generally a spender of income derived from the productive activities of private citizens and businesses. Citizens and businesses as providers of funding and governments as administrators who oversee delivery of services have to work together to realize joint goals of providing adequate public infrastructure and social services, a prerequisite for sustainable economic growth.

Governments rely on citizens and businesses for tax revenue. When government spending plans exceed its revenue collections, there is a budget or fiscal deficit. The deficit is often filled by borrowing or raising additional tax revenue. When government expenditure plans far exceed revenue collections, the large amounts of borrowing required to plug the deficit may impose a considerable long-term tax burden on citizens. Large amounts of borrowing is not a sustainable funding solution for providing public services.

The provision of public services and social benefits is only sustainable when it is affordable in terms of the willingness and ability of citizens to pay. When a government borrows to fund the provision of public services that its citizens cannot afford, it creates an unsustainable short-term gain (service availability) but builds the potential for economic pain several years down the road. Citizens may be worse-off than if the unaffordable (but highly desirable) service or social benefit was never provided. However, because of near-term incentives for getting elected or staying in office, governments can be tempted to finance the delivery of certain benefits or services through excessive borrowing that can become a burden for future generations. Informed citizens are more likely to reject such "short-term gain with long-term pain" policies in favour of more sustainable solutions.

In some cases, expanding public infrastructure and social services may be an efficient way for the government to redistribute wealth within the economy. In a bid to promote the welfare of its citizens, especially in cases where sources of income in an economy are heavily skewed towards particular sectors or regions, the provision of public infrastructure and social services and the associated employment opportunities may be an efficient way for the government to redistribute income in the economy.

Rather than redistributing income directly to citizens, a government may target the expansion of public services such as education and healthcare in deprived communities, in a bid to improve living standards. In addition to the welfare enhancing impact of these services, wages of local public sector employees can expand the size of the local economy and stimulate other economic initiatives. This model of government redistribution can be healthy, as long as, it is affordable and does not excessively distort incentives in the private sector. In countries where a considerable proportion of economic output and government revenues are derived from capital intensive extractive industries, such as mining or oil production, public sector employment can be an effective avenue for income redistribution.

In a democracy, citizens share greater responsibility for economic and social outcomes. Citizens are ultimately responsible for the availability and quality of public infrastructure and social services. Adequate public infrastructure is desirable but costly. Citizens are responsible for footing the cost and the government is responsible for administering the service. An effective government will strive to deliver more and better public services with fewer resources, that is, exhibit a high level of government productivity. A responsible citizen will be more proactive in engaging in economic activity, paying taxes, and monitoring government administration to ensure greater efficiency. A government that fails to provide adequate public infrastructure and services, primarily because its citizens are not productive enough and hence do not supply sufficient tax revenue should not take the full blame for the infrastructure/service deficit. The willingness and ability of citizens to pay for desirable public services ultimately sets limits to the scope and quality of services that governments can provide.

Governments are often easy targets for public infrastructure deficits or poor economic developments, two areas where they have significant influence over results. However, in functioning democracies, citizens are given the power to effectively choose governments and their policies; therefore, they are ultimately responsible for economic and social outcomes. Citizens have the power to change a government whose policies go against the welfare of the people or when they lose confidence in the efficiency of public administration (e.g. due to corruption or poor service standards).

Almost all elected governments and political parties have the same long-term goal—to improve the welfare of their citizens. The main difference between political parties and governments often lies with their different views about the most sustainable path to reach this ultimate goal. Many government policy initiatives have the greatest impact over the long-term when the government who initiated the policy may be out of office.

In functioning democracies, citizens are ultimately responsible for economic and social outcomes.

The incentives of an elected government are not always aligned to the welfare of citizens. Elected governments are primarily concerned about staying in office. Political parties live to win elections. That is their number one objective and this self-interest is not necessarily aligned to the welfare of citizens at all times. The short-term of office for most elected governments (four to five years, or two cycles of eight to ten years) and their obsession with staying elected can create moral hazard problems for society. In order to stay elected, a government may have strong incentives to favor policies that provide desirable short-term benefits but that may ultimately work against citizens' long-term interests. The presence of this moral-hazard problem, is the primary reason why citizens should take up responsibility for monitoring government policies. For example, an elected government may be tempted to increase spending on public services to gain favour with voters. Unchecked government spending may destroy the prospects of businesses and individuals (primary sources of government tax revenue) and create broader economic problems. However, the short-term horizon of elected governments may push them to increase spending anyway, in order to create an illusion of gain or benefits that will help the government win elections. The ability of a government to create and benefit from such illusions of gain is primarily dependent on the ignorance of citizens about the economic relationship they have with their governments.

The short-term political incentives of elected governments may put them under pressure to create illusions of gain that may ultimately work against the welfare of the public. Citizens need to be proactive in monitoring government policy in order to safeguard their long-term interests.

The business of government is far too important to be left entirely in the hands of elected governors. The role of government and the influence of government policy on the welfare of citizens are too important to be left unmonitored. In most countries, individuals, businesses, and other stakeholders have the privilege of representing their interests to elected officials. Smart entrepreneurs and business owners proactively exercise their rights (rights that all citizens share) to influence government policy (in their favour). Business owners exercise this right because they have strong and direct economic incentives to do so. In order to maximize the welfare of any society, citizens need to take a more proactive role in monitoring governance practices. Society can only guarantee the nurturing of effective leadership by providing a framework that encourages citizens to develop greater interest in understanding the business of government, the resources required and costs involved in delivering adequate public infrastructure and social services, and the impact of government policy on households, businesses, and the broader economy.

In a democracy, citizens are ultimately responsible for determining how they are governed. A society that gives individuals the right to vote (essentially the right to make policy choices) without first educating them about the workings of government and the economic and social link between the state and the citizen may not reap the full potential benefits of a democracy. Greater knowledge about the economic link between citizens and their governments could help citizens make more informed election decisions and promote policies that are better aligned to their welfare.

Governments are sensitive to feedback from their citizens. A progressive society needs to have a strong link between a government and its citizens. Each party needs to take up its responsibility in order to achieve their common desired goals in the long term. Interestingly, every government is made up of citizens. A healthy and responsible relationship between citizens and the government would encourage competent citizens to step up and take interest in the business of governing, exercise their voting rights more responsibly, and take a more active role in monitoring government policy decisions and providing feedback. Feedback on policy discussions and policy decisions do matter, and governments all over the world, respond to it.

Citizens have an economic incentive to be vigilant and scrutinize government policies, because they ultimately pay the price. Elected governments should also be vigilant and only accept mandates that a government can have an advantage in executing. For example, in many developing nations, governments accept a mandate to be the main provider of formal employment opportunities in the economy, a policy that could cripple private economic initiatives in the long term. On the contrary, a government could achieve better and more sustainable long-term employment objectives by creating stable economic conditions that allows private enterprise to flourish (e.g. by delivering an environment of low and stable inflation and interest rates). Responsible citizens should be more circumspect about endorsing unsustainable policies that provide illusions of welfare improvement in the short-term. For example, if a government decides to materially increase public sector employee wages, cut utility prices, or pursue other measures that appear to be welfare enhancing in the short term, how should a responsible citizen react to such policies? A good understanding of the economic relationship between a government and its people would dictate that in making a decision, citizens should compare the value of the promised benefits to the additional costs that they are likely to bear as taxpayers in the future. Policies must be analyzed for their long-term impact on the welfare of citizens.

Taxes

Taxes form the basis of a strong economic link between citizens and governments. Governments impose both direct and indirect taxes on citizens to raise revenue. Direct taxes are more obvious and increase incentives for citizens to take greater responsibility to monitor. Tax payments are required by law; failure to pay can be a punishable crime.

Governments provide the most efficient means to deliver certain important welfare improving services. Just as citizens happily and willingly pay out-of-pocket to improve their welfare by buying individual consumption items (e.g., restaurant meals, cars, groceries, etc.) they should be equally interested in paying taxes to support the provision of essential public services that improve their welfare. In functioning democracies, the opportunity for citizens to monitor and influence how tax resources are used should also increase incentives for people to pay taxes.

Direct taxes are imposed on people, businesses, or assets. Examples of direct taxes include tax on property and other real estate, tax on individual income, tax on business profits, and a wealth tax on assets of individuals and businesses. Direct taxes are transparent, and people are more aware of how much they pay. Because the payment of direct taxes are more obvious, they raise a higher level of consciousness among citizens of their responsibility for tax payment. Direct taxes are therefore more likely to induce stronger democratic engagement from citizens to demand efficient use of their tax contributions.

In some developing countries a meaningful proportion of economic activity and jobs may be informal (jobs are not formally registered, and income is not formally declared). Many businesses and workers either pay low or no income tax. Governments in these countries tend to favour the collection of indirect taxes but can also employ and enforce other forms of direct tax (e.g., property tax) so that each household becomes better aware of its tax responsibilities. Even in countries dominated by formal employment opportunities, it is the responsibility of the employer to deduct income tax from employee salaries (on behalf of the government). As a result, income tax may sometimes be seen as an indirect cost to the employer rather than a direct cost to the employee, who focuses mostly on his take-home pay. Direct taxes such as property tax or wealth tax are paid out of pocket and can be more effective in inducing democratic engagement because, people are more conscious of paying them. Direct taxes are more progressive; people with higher income and wealth often contribute a higher proportion of tax (relative to their income levels).

Indirect or consumption taxes are levied on consumption and expenditure. They are imposed on transactions of goods and services and are typically embedded in the price such that consumers may not be aware of how much they are paying in tax. Indirect taxes include custom duties on imports; excise duties on gasoline, tobacco, luxury goods, and other products; sales tax; and value-added tax. Indirect taxes increase the final price of consumer goods. In most countries, the sticker prices on goods fully reflect the impact of indirect taxes. The seller of the good collects the tax on behalf of the government and the buyer who only sees the sticker price may not be aware of his tax responsibilities and can typically not identify the amount of tax embedded in the sticker price. Because indirect taxes are less obvious, governments are tempted to increase them whenever there is a need for greater tax revenue. Because citizens are less aware of the tax and the amounts involved, indirect taxes are less likely to generate adverse reaction from citizens and do not create strong incentives to monitor. Indirect taxes are regressive taxes because they are not charged in proportion to one's income level or ability to pay. The tax rate applies to the value of the good rather than the income of the buyer. All consumers buying the same good pay exactly the same amount of tax. As a result, lower-income consumers pay a higher rate of tax (relative to their income).

*****

POLICIES THAT CAN CREATE STRONG INCENTIVES FOR CITIZENS TO MONITOR AND TAKE GREATER RESPONSIBILITY FOR GOVERNANCE STANDARDS

Policies that encourage higher levels of economic participation among citizens can improve incentives to monitor and support higher governance standards. Higher levels of economic engagement as business owners, employees, property owners, direct-tax payers and owners of financial assets among the voting population raise incentives of citizens to monitor government policy and make more informed election choices. Higher levels of economic participation among citizens may contribute to increase knowledge about how businesses create value and how this translates into their capacity to provide sustainable employment opportunities. Higher levels of economic participation increases public knowledge about the impact of government economic policy on household income and wealth.

A broad application of taxes, particularly direct taxes. Taxes form an essential economic link between the citizen and the state, and progressive citizens should see the payment of taxes as an opportunity to contribute towards the provision of necessary public infrastructure and social services.

The payment of direct taxes provides strong incentives to monitor government polices to ensure that they serve the welfare of the taxpayer. Throughout history, tax demands on citizens have induced local communities all around the world to demand improvements in public services, wider political representation, and greater economic and social freedom. The legal requirement to pay taxes has the potential to induce greater activism among citizens; historically it has been instrumental in entrenching democratic rights and privileges around the world. For example, during the mid-eighteenth century, in reaction to higher taxes imposed by England on the American colonies, residents of Boston successfully championed a "No Taxation without Representation" policy that ultimately contributed to the greater goal of independence from England.

In essence, paying taxes provides authority to the right of citizens to have a say in how they are governed. A broad application of direct taxes can help to create a stronger economic link between citizens and the government.

Low levels of direct taxation weaken the economic link between citizens and the government and lowers incentives for citizens to monitor. In some resource-rich countries, the majority of government revenue does not come directly from the economic activities of average citizens. It is primarily derived from a few large companies and a fraction of the working population. This situation weakens the economic link between the average citizen and the government and reduces incentives to monitor. In these countries, the government is seen as the controller of national wealth that pours from natural resources, which few people are involved in developing and citizens become dependants of the state, focused on receiving benefits. Citizens have few economic incentives to internalize their responsibility to engage and monitor in order to ensure adequate governance standards. In countries where the economic activities of private citizens do not contribute meaningfully to government finances, the relationship between the citizen and the state may be more parasitic than symbiotic, and the long-term consequences on governance and living standards could be suboptimal.

Poor governance practices are more likely in countries where governments tend not to require or enforce direct taxes on citizens because of the fear of public revolt against such taxes. The absence of a strong incentive for citizens to monitor government activities provides a "free license" to a government to serve its own interests, which may come at the expense of public welfare. In many countries with weak governance standards, citizens and the government appear to exist in parallel spheres. The government's obligation to the citizen is weak, because public finances are not largely influenced by the economic activities of the average citizen. Without the active payment of taxes, a citizen's right to make demands on the government or seek better governance standards may also be weak.

In countries where there is a stronger link between the economic activities of citizens and government finances, citizens are more likely to embrace their tax responsibilities and be more proactive in monitoring how the government spends public finances. In the same way that paying directly for a service increases one's vested interest in making demands on service quality, direct tax payments create a stronger economic incentive to monitor governance standards. Countries with stronger tax links between the average citizen and the state tend to have more adequate levels of public services, more stable economies, and higher governance standards.

Greater information about the cost of public services can improve the efficiency of use, improve willingness to pay, and increase demands on service quality. Price discovery has an impact on how people use resources. Price discovery can help citizens make more efficient use of public services. Public services are typically not accompanied by price information (sometimes for very healthy social reasons). True price discovery may also be limited through the impact of government subsidies. For example, in many countries, the government funds public education and healthcare, two long-term investments that deliver immense social and economic benefits. By effectively lowering or eliminating the direct out-of-pocket cost of these services, utilization could become less efficient. Because they are subsidized to be cheaper or "free," people may consume higher than "normal" levels or make suboptimal use of these services. Public services are not free for society; they are costly to provide and take up a significant proportion of tax revenue.

By providing citizens with information on the true economic cost of public services, even if the final out-of-pocket cost remains unchanged, there is a possibly that people may use public services more efficiently, take greater interest in paying taxes, and make higher demands on service quality. For example, if students received a bill at the end of every term that showed how much taxpayers paid to provide their education, this information might prompt students to take their education more seriously. Parents who are ultimately paying for the cost of public education through their tax contributions, may have stronger incentives to demand higher education standards. Such price information would also send a powerful message about the high cost associated with the delivery of public services and inspire citizens to be more proactive taxpayers. Disclosure of detailed cost information on public services, can also induce stronger scrutiny of the cost effectiveness of service delivery.

Efficient feedback mechanisms can improve the effectiveness of government administration. Policies based on good intentions may sometimes have unintended negative consequences. Mechanisms that encourage constructive scrutiny and feedback to businesses, governments, and other decision makers have the potential to lead to better allocation and management of resources. In countries with well-developed capital markets, the private sector has the potential to allocate resources more efficiently. Capital markets employ paid investment professionals who provide independent feedback on investment decisions of firms, as part of their mandate to safeguard the interest of capital providers (savers). A government has the legal ability to raise money through taxes and does not need to appeal to its citizens to fund specific projects. There are no established professional bodies who represent the interest of citizens by providing independent feedback on government policy decisions. However, because the consequences of government action (or inappropriate action) are so relevant to the welfare of citizens and businesses, they all share a responsibility to monitor and provide feedback. High levels of economic participation and greater ownership of financial assets can provide citizens with independent information about the impact of government policies on their welfare and support more efficient feedback transmission mechanisms.

Adequate levels of education (including education on civic values) may improve the ability and willingness of citizens to monitor. There is a danger that, if left without proper scrutiny, elected governments may spend national resources in serving their own interests rather than the interest of citizens who elected them and who ultimately pay for public services. The moral-hazard problem may be universal, but strong levels of education—including an adequate level of education on civic values— can help improve the ability of citizens to effectively monitor against potential misalignment of interests. Good governance is not error-free, but it does involve avoiding unsustainable practices that carry negative long-term consequences for citizens. Educated citizens who have the ability to understand how their individual economic prospects are linked to government policies can often provide more objective feedback to their government and support governance standards that are better aligned to public welfare.

Greater access to information about the costs and benefits associated with government policies from a number of independent sources can support the ability of citizens to monitor and improve the quality of governance. Every benefit or service that the government provides has costs associated with it. There may be a significant disconnect between what people say they want and how their decisions might change if they had to pay directly for it. To help citizens make more informed choices, it is important for the government and other stakeholders, such as businesses, academics, and activists, to detail their understanding of costs and benefits associated with key policy initiatives. Policy makers have a duty to study the demands of citizens, to educate them about the costs involved in meeting these demands, and to show how costs are to be split among citizens (because citizens ultimately foot the bill). Broader access to information from independent sources can help citizens to make more responsible choices. A responsible government will justify major policy decisions and ask for feedback from private citizens and businesses, the ultimate financiers and beneficiaries of these policy actions.

Well-developed financial markets have the potential to stimulate stronger economic incentives for citizens to monitor government policy. In countries that have well-developed financial markets, there is wider ownership of financial assets such as stocks, bonds, and debt-financed personal property. Sustainable government policy can create an environment of low interest rates, which makes it possible for the majority of households to take long-term loans (mortgage loans) from banks to buy houses. In countries where pensions have been privatized, direct pension-contribution schemes work like individual "savings accounts": the pension savings contributed by both individuals and their employers are invested in funds that hold shares and bonds of companies as well as government bonds.

When people own financial assets directly, they take greater interest in the prospects of businesses and the economy in general. Government economic policies have an observable impact on the value of financial assets and liabilities. This link is too obvious and too strong for households to ignore. The objectivity of the information makes it less susceptible to political manipulation and ultimately creates incentives for better governance that serves the long-term interest of citizens.

When the average citizen has an economic stake in financial assets, the power of financial markets to induce people to monitor is partly derived from the fact that the value of people's investments readily adjusts to incorporate new information. The interest rates on loans that citizens take from banks can be directly affected by changes in government policy. When the government enacts prudent economic policies, the economic prospects of private citizens (individuals, households, and businesses) are likely to improve. An improvement in economic opportunities for firms and households tends to support higher prices of financial assets. On the other hand, poor economic policies and excessive government borrowing can cripple the economic prospects of businesses, raise the level of interest rates, and depress the value of financial assets. Households with mortgage loans may suffer steep falls in affordability levels, when interest rates rise sharply. Financial markets can be so efficient that interest rates and prices of financial assets can often adjust in response to policy announcements even before the policies are signed into law. The ability of financial instruments to calibrate the welfare impact of economic policies and offer objective and timely feedback to citizens can help create stronger incentives for citizens to monitor government policy and improve the quality of feedback.

Respectable and powerful institutions such as banks, the military, and corporations are normally headed by well-informed professionals who have great knowledge of what it takes to lead such institutions. However, because people in power can sometimes be tempted to put their own interests above that of those who they are meant to serve, all of these institutions are actively monitored by direct beneficiaries, independent regulatory bodies, or governments. The government is the most powerful institution in any country, and the monitoring role of citizens is crucial to maintain the alignment of interest.

The economic link between a government and its people: a horse-racing analogy. Elected governments are comparable to strong and powerful racehorses. The best results (i.e., the creation of a prosperous and harmonious society), require not only the selection of the strongest and fastest breeds of racehorses (i.e., electing the most capable officials) but also requires a good jockey (the responsible citizen) to hold the reigns and keep the horse in check (i.e. to monitor).

NEW OPPORTUNITIES TO STRUCTURALLY IMPROVE POLITICAL REPRESENTATION IN THE TWENTY-FIRST CENTURY

In current times, the rise of mobile-phone technology and online access throughout the world, has the potential to improve political representation. Our legacy governance architecture, where most decisions are taken by elected representatives on behalf of citizens, could be complemented by higher levels of direct representation from citizens. The current system of elected representatives has been inherited from times when average education levels were low and travel costs so high that it was practically impossible for citizens to directly represent their interests or voice their opinions on key policies. Given technological advancement in recent years, this system can be enhanced by active and timely online surveys of citizens' views on key policies. Technology makes it possible to seek the views of citizens readily and at a negligible cost. Getting the populace more involved on a regular basis increases incentives for people to monitor government policy and creates a stronger alignment of interests between the governors and the governed. Broadening the depth of representation to include the direct views of citizens has the potential to promote better governance by reducing risks associated with embedding so much power in an elected representative. The excessive power that elected representatives wield, provides greater opportunities for corruption, the pledge of votes to buy political favour or earn financial support, and the active lobbying by large corporations to influence policies in their favour. These risks are major challenges to all democracies because they can influence government policies to favour a few interested parties (with strong incentives) at the expense of the welfare of the general public. Technology has made it possible, for the first time in history, to bring true and direct representation to the door of every citizen.

CHAPTER 7

THE ROLE OF THE GOVERNMENT IN THE ECONOMY
STATE VS PRIVATE CAPITAL

We who live in free market societies believe that growth, prosperity and, ultimately, human fulfilment are created from the bottom up, not the government down. Only when the human spirit is allowed to invent and create, only when individuals are given a personal stake in deciding economic policies and benefiting from their success—only then can societies remain alive, dynamic, prosperous, progressive and free. Trust the people.
—Ronald Reagan (1911–2004), fortieth President of the United States.

THE GOVERNMENT IS RESPONSIBLE FOR MANAGING THE ECONOMY

In managing the economy to promote growth and stability, a government's economic policy should complement the initiatives of private citizens. For example, a progressive government that aims to cushion the effect of economic cycles will contain government spending in periods of strong economic growth, when individuals and businesses enjoy favourable prospects, and deploy the savings to stimulate economic activity and expand employment opportunities in times of slower growth, when consumer and investor confidence is low. A government that overspends in periods of strong economic growth, when businesses and workers face attractive prospects and pay more taxes due to stronger earnings, may find itself in a position to cut spending and directly contribute to further dampen economic conditions in periods of slower growth.

Erratic changes in economic policy and general regulatory uncertainty can to depress economic growth by reducing the ability of individuals and businesses to undertake long-term investment projects. Countries that experience high levels of economic instability are more likely to have high levels of unemployment, social unrest, and political instability. Every economy goes through cycles. However, the government's management of the economy can be instrumental is smoothing-out these cycles and reducing their frequency. Prudent economic management can support longer periods of economic growth and reduce the duration of weak economic conditions.

Every economy goes through cycles. However, the government's management of the economy can be instrumental is smoothing-out these cycles and reducing their frequency.

79

Government spending power can enable the creation of a considerable number of jobs and support the growth of many industries. However, excessive government spending can ruin the economy by driving up interest rates and making it difficult or impossible for private citizens and business to borrow or attract capital for investment. By controlling its spending habits, in relation to its revenue, the government can have a meaningful impact on interest rates and economic stability.

The central bank is the government institution that controls the amount of money that is readily available in the economy. By controlling the money supply and therefore the value of money, the central bank has great influence over the rate of price increases in the economy. An environment of stable prices encourages citizens and businesses to save and invest in long-term opportunities. An environment of high price increases (high inflation) creates great uncertainty for citizens and often erodes their affordability (purchasing power) for goods and services. High interest rates are more likely to prevail in countries with high inflation. High interest rates increase the cost of borrowing for citizens and businesses and restrict their ability to invest. Through its regulatory role and ability to provide funding to banks and other financial institutions, the central bank has a major influence on the willingness of financial institutions to lend. By controlling money supply growth and influencing the cost of funds in the economy, central bank policies have a meaningful impact on economic stability and growth.

Countries that are major exporters of commodities may be prone to higher levels of economic instability (more frequent and deeper cycles) due to volatility in commodity prices. When a significant source of government revenue is derived from commodities, sharp changes in commodity prices can have a meaningful impact on the government's ability to carry about key investment initiatives. However, even in such countries, there is considerable scope for governments to employ prudent economic policies to lessen the impact of commodity cycles. In periods of rising commodity prices, such countries may experience unusually strong increases in government revenue and foreign exchange earnings. It may be prudent to save part of the "bumper" revenues and foreign exchange earnings. Such savings can be used to reduce debt and build up foreign exchange reserves to stimulate the economy when commodity prices fall sharply. A government that is too eager to spend strong revenues derived from rising commodity prices may be forced to make deep cuts to government spending in periods of falling commodity prices.

Globalization and government credibility. Elected governments often credit themselves with strong economic and employment growth, even in situations where regional or global factors may have been the key growth driver. Governments are however quicker to apportion responsibility for difficult economic conditions on external factors. Due to growing global interdependence, citizens need to assess a country's economic performance not in isolation but relative to its relevant peers (which may be regional peers or countries with a comparable economic structure), in order to isolate the effects of global or regional factors. Relative economic performance among relevant peers, rather than absolute performance, can provide a more useful indication of the effectiveness of a government's economic policy. One has to consider external factors (both negative and positive) and the effectiveness of the policy response to these factors in assessing the economic performance of a government.

A government's credibility on economic management can be instrumental in stimulating economic activity, particularly in periods of low confidence and uncertainty. Economic growth is the result of the collective action of every citizen, business, and the government. When governments and public institutions have gained credibility from a long track record of prudently managing an economy, the populace is more likely to trust the government to be honest about the economic outlook and implement policies that promote economic stability and sustainable growth. The value of this trust and the confidence that it can inspire can be instrumental in stimulating economic activity in periods of uncertainty.

In an economic downturn, activity levels decline because of great uncertainty about employment prospects for workers, and revenue and profit prospects for firms. Individuals and businesses who are interested in purchasing goods for consumption or investment purposes may cancel or defer their purchasing decisions because of the weak economic outlook. For example, a worker with a healthy income who is interested in buying a new house or a car, may become more cautious and withhold spending, when he sees other people losing their jobs. As more people defer or cancel their spending and investment plans, the economy becomes more likely to remain weak or weaken further. The ability of credible governments and institutions (such as central banks) to cushion the psychological impact of a downturn by imbuing confidence in the face of uncertainty is perhaps one of the most important roles of the government in an economy. Government credibility is earned over a long period of prudent economic management. In countries where credibility is lacking, government efforts to inspire confidence in periods of high economic uncertainty has a limited impact, and in some cases, policies aimed at restoring confidence could trigger adverse reactions due to a legacy of poor policy decisions under such challenging conditions.

The ability of credible governments and institutions (such as central banks) to cushion the psychological impact of a downturn by inspiring confidence in the face of uncertainty is one of the most important roles of the government in an economy.

Integrity is a strong foundation for good governance and economic management. The impact of prudent economic policies is often reflected in a number of economic indicators that often move in the same direction. Governments that abuse their monopoly over the supply of money to finance excessive government spending ultimately drive up prices and erode the purchasing power of their citizens. Governments that spend beyond their means and borrow excessively, create large tax burdens on their citizens and raise the cost of borrowing for households and businesses. Governments that promise unsustainable benefits in order to meet short-term political goals ultimately heap great costs on their citizens over the long term. Without a track record of integrity, citizens are less likely to trust their governments, and government economic policies become less effective.

While economic growth is important, policies that try to generate growth through disingenuous means are unlikely to improve living standards in the long-term. Some governments are notorious for attempting to employ disingenuous means in an attempt to stimulate economic growth. For example, a government may finance large increases in public-sector investment spending and employment growth by printing money or borrowing excessively. Such financing measures may impose significant tax burdens on citizens and depress their purchasing power and living standards over the long-term. In countries with such governments, one has to be circumspect in evaluating reported economic growth figures. Under certain situations, even as government reports suggest the presence of economic growth, it is possible for the purchasing power and living standards of citizens to decline sharply when incomes are assessed on an independent basis—for example, in terms of their affordability for basic goods and services—or when a more stable currency is used as the basis for measuring income levels. Globalization of product markets implies that policies that have an adverse impact on the exchange rate of a country's currency (in relation to currencies used for international trade such as the U.S. dollar), may sharply reduce the purchasing power of citizens (or residents). Sustainable economic growth has to be derived from policies that support increases in productivity.

The credibility derived from prudent management of an economy pays an attractive long-term dividend to deserving governments and their citizens. A government that has earned the trust of citizens in its management of the economy also earns a sustainable right to a larger credit line (higher capacity for government borrowing relative to GDP) and the ability to borrow money for very long periods (ten, twenty, and thirty years) at low interest rates. Such generous credit terms can support the ability of the government to undertake long-term investments. An environment of low interest rates on government borrowings creates favourable conditions for households and businesses to borrow at attractive rates to finance long-term investments such as housing or business expansion projects.

A government's management of the economy and spending plans could be more challenging in countries with high levels of poverty, income inequality and a high level of dependence on the state. In a democracy, the incentives of different segments of the population may not be aligned. In countries where large proportions of the population are poor and more likely to be beneficiaries of government welfare programs, their voting power may tilt government policy in favour of larger welfare programs and greater government intervention to provide services at subsidized prices, even when these practices are not sustainable. In countries where the government and government controlled companies are the largest employers in the economy, the strong bargaining power of public sector employees may put pressure on the government to cater to their interests above those of all other citizens. On the other hand, in countries where private businesses are collectively responsible for creating the majority of formal employment opportunities as well as the most attractive job opportunities, citizens may be more likely to support economic policies that empower private firms and households to shoulder responsibility for economic growth and job creation.

CONSIDERATIONS FOR SETTING LIMITS TO STATE CAPITAL IN THE ECONOMY

The government has such massive financial resources and legal powers that it is nearly impossible or extremely challenging for private citizens and businesses to compete against the state in the production of goods and services. In countries where there is strong popular support for government intervention in the economy. The tentacles of the state can permeate many sectors of the economy. Government controlled firms may dominate the provision of services such as education, healthcare, banking, extractive industries (such as mining and oil production), manufacturing, food retail, air travel, and may monopolize pension assets and utility services.

In order to maximize the welfare of the general public, citizens (voters) may need to carefully define and limit the role of state capital in the economy. It may be necessary to reserve certain economic opportunities for private citizens especially in activities where private capital and greater competition result in superior solutions. To promote the welfare of the public, the government should restrict its activities to areas where it has a strong advantage relative to the private sector. When the state dominates economic activity in many sectors, the lack of competition may limit service quality and consumer choice, and reduce productivity and innovation.

Excessive government involvement in an economy may generate significant hidden costs that stem from lower levels of efficiency. Governments may be under political pressure to reduce the direct out-of-pocket cost of services that they provide. Because subsidies have the potential to distort resource allocation decisions, they can increase the total cost of service delivery. Penalties associated with excessive government intervention in the economy may include limits on consumer choice and service quality; higher taxes on households and businesses; a higher cost of borrowing (interest rates) for the government which is essentially a further tax on citizens; higher cost of borrowing for household and businesses; and reduced opportunities for private citizens to express their initiatives.

Excessive involvement of the government in the economy may crowd-out initiatives of private citizens and saddle them with a significant tax burden. Excessive government intervention in the economy reduces competition and limits consumer choice.

Enabling greater economic opportunities for private citizens can be welfare-enhancing because, in a world of uncertainty, the effectiveness of millions of individual economic decision makers can be far greater than that of one powerful centralized planner (the government). In countries where economic activity and employment are dominated by state companies and government decisions, there is essentially one key decision maker in the economy, and everyone obsesses over the decision maker getting it right. Citizens are constantly preoccupied with government-policy decisions because such policies can make or break the economic prospects and living standards of large portions of the population. Wisdom, humility, and historical evidence dictate that in an uncertain world, the collective efforts of individual decision-makers who are guided by an innate ambition to improve their well-being can be more effective in reacting to challenges and taking advantage of opportunities. People have a strong natural inclination to seek opportunities that improve their welfare. The amalgamation of millions of independent naturally induced welfare enhancing initiatives can be far more powerful in improving the well-being of the whole society; it cannot be rivaled by the wisest decisions of a single individual or a small body of representatives.

A progressive government would enact policies that empower private initiative. Wherever it is possible, a government should empower citizens to provide for themselves rather than empower itself to provide for citizens. People react to incentives. A merit-based society that allows individuals the freedom to innovate, work hard, and earn the fruits of their labour is more likely to prosper than a society that blunts incentives for individual initiative. An economy underpinned by millions of independent decision-makers who are naturally incentivized to refine and adapt their decisions on a daily basis to seek the most optimal results is more likely to deliver sustainable growth that an economy that relies on a single—and inherently slow—key decision-maker.

A progressive government needs to understand and stick to delivery of services that are most efficient for a government to provide. The government is the most efficient provider of a large number of public services such as national security, judicial services, public roads and the provision of regulatory oversight for many industries. For many of these services, the government's advantage stems from the fact that a profit motive, a precondition for private sector interest, fails to maximize the welfare of the general public. However in the broader economy, the profit-seeking motive of private citizens has the potential to create far superior welfare gains for the whole society. This is because competition among private firms stimulates innovation and productivity gains. Competition links gains in public welfare to the financial rewards of innovative and productive firms. It creates a more sustainable platform for advancing social welfare.

Notwithstanding their inherent power and influence, governments ought to be circumspect and humble enough to relinquish responsibility for providing services in sectors where competition has the potential to deliver superior results. For example, in the telecommunications sector in many developing countries, government monopolies had struggled for decades to provide services to small segments of the population. However, since opening up the market for private-sector participation, competition among more efficient private providers has attracted significant investment and increased the quality and availability of telecommunications services at more competitive prices. For example, supported by the rapid pace of private investment, the number of phone subscribers in Africa increased from about 10 million in the year 2000 to over 600 million by 2010.

When the government dominates economic activity, it is likely to become the most influential employer in many industries. Government dominance in the labour market may distort productivity incentives and reduce overall employment opportunities in the economy. When state capital is active in many sectors of the economy, the government can become the largest formal employer in most sectors of the economy. The concentration of jobs within one employer whose incentives are better aligned to the promotion of employee welfare than productivity, can lead to the payment of higher-than-market wages to public-sector employees. When a large and influential employer pays higher than market wages, this has the potential to distort incentives in the labour market and reduce employment opportunities in the economy.

When the government dominates formal employment opportunities and sets wages above competitive market levels, its welfare initiatives may indirectly increase the cost of hiring for other employers. Higher-than-market wages for public sector employees are clearly beneficial to those employees but may come at a high long-term cost to society. Private employers who face a high cost of hiring workers may have fewer resources to expand. The private sector is more competitive; it creates stronger incentives to stimulate innovation and advances in employee productivity. When the government has an unfair advantage in tapping the talent pool in an economy, depleted human-capital resources for the private sector may lower the level of innovation and job-creation potential in the overall economy.

Higher-than-market wages for public-sector employees may contribute to higher levels of unemployment, because (qualified) workers may prefer to concentrate their efforts on lobbying and preparing for opportunities to work for the government than take up readily available, lower-wage job opportunities in the private sector. In extreme cases, public-sector jobs become comparable to lottery tickets, where the few winners are destined to receive generous salaries that command high purchasing power for the rest of their lives, but losers are condemned to permanently finance payment to the winners through their tax contributions. When the government sets a high bar for wages (beyond the means of most private employers), some skilled workers who are not able to access jobs with comparable wages may become discouraged and leave the labour force.

When the government is the largest provider of formal jobs in the economy, public-sector employees may become a very large and powerful union with strong political influence. Their collective bargaining power and control over key services can bring the government and the economy to a standstill, in the event of a strike. Their concentrated voting power has the potential to make them a powerful voting bloc within a country. For political reasons, governments in these situations may sometimes be pressured to undertake policies that promote the interest of public-sector employees, often at the expense of the general public.

In countries where the government is the dominant employer in the economy, public sector employee unions may wield strong political influence which may sometimes be employed to advance their own interests at the expense of the general public.'

Political incentives may distort the ability of governments to allocate capital efficiently in the provision of revenue-generating services. Because the government is not a profit-maximizing entity, there may be a perception that government provision of revenue-generating services, such as utility services, has to be better or less costly for citizens. However, political incentives may distort the ability of the government to charge a fair price for these services or maintain an efficient cost base. Political interference in service delivery may weaken the ability of the government to provide these services on a sustainable basis.

Government intervention to subsidize the true cost of services can lead to inefficiencies in the allocation of resources. A government may sometimes lower the price of utilities below their true economic cost in order to win short-term political favour. Distorting prices leads to less efficient allocation of resources, and citizens may ultimately face undesirable long-term consequences from such seemingly generous short-term measures. When prices are set below the sustainable cost of production, the lower prices can lead to overconsumption and under-investment. Service availability and service quality may suffer after long periods of under-investment. In many countries, the decision to hand over the provision of utility services to private companies (from the government) is often due to inadequate service quality and large gaps in service availability.

Inefficiencies associated with government intervention in the economy may carry high hidden costs. For example, the electricity-generation sector in a number of developing countries remains under government control. The result is that, for political reasons, power tariffs are often kept low and below the cost of sustainable production and investment. In many of these countries, electricity supply is limited and erratic, which creates a major hurdle for economic growth and employment. Individuals and businesses who resort to alternative sources of power from diesel generators incur costs that are many times higher than the true economic cost of generating power on an industrial scale. Economic activity and job creation suffer because, presumably, the government cares so much about the welfare of its people that it tries to protect them from rising utility costs. The true economic cost of government intervention in this case goes beyond the tariffs people are asked to pay. The true cost to users has to include the electricity tariffs, lost hours of work because of power cuts, lost job creation opportunities, lost investment, lost business revenue and profits, and missed opportunities for additional government revenue. These hidden costs are likely to exceed the perceived benefit that citizens may be receiving from government subsidies.

Political incentives create major challenges for maintaining cost competitiveness. Maintaining an efficient cost base is a major challenge for all firms but can be particularly difficult for the government. Elected governments are in the business of staying in power. Laying off unproductive workers or reducing the number of employees because of gains in technology that make it feasible to deliver more services with fewer employees are hard decisions for governments to make. Laying off public-sector workers may carry high political penalties. Furthermore, when an industry is in decline because of new technology, government control typically means that the industry and its employees will survive much longer than could be economically justified. When the government employs more people than is necessary to deliver a service, it ultimately raises the cost paid by consumers and businesses in the form of higher taxes (and/or poor service quality) even when the product price is kept artificially low.

The risk of corruption may rise when the government controls a considerable amount of investment spending in the economy. In some countries, the government is by far the largest investor in many sectors of the economy. The concentration of spending power within one key decision maker can increase the risk of corruption. Compared to private companies, where a strong ownership mentality creates incentives for efficiency (cost savings) in an effort to maximize profits, the government may have fewer direct incentives for cost savings. When the government controls large amounts of investment spending, supplying services to the government becomes a major business opportunity. Firms that win large government contracts may be rewarded with the opportunity to earn extraordinary profits. Because the profit opportunity can be so large, firms are more likely to use bribes and political connections to influence government decisions in their favour. By employing political favor to reduce competition for government contracts, politically connected firms can inflate the cost of service delivery and earn even larger profits. Corruption inflates the cost of providing services; it is effectively an additional tax on citizens. Corruption further distorts economic incentives in a country. When the opportunity for earning large profits is not linked to firms that deliver the best services at the most competitive prices, there may be little incentives for firms and employees to innovate or invest in productivity enhancing initiatives. By raising the cost of services and destroying incentives for productivity, corruption stifles the potential for economic growth and reduces living standards.

Elected governments can better enhance the welfare of citizens by encouraging competition among private service providers while maintaining regulatory oversight. An elected government's political interest in staying elected may create a conflict of interest in operating revenue-generating services. It may be more prudent for the government to allocate the provision of revenue-generating services to private companies and maintain regulatory oversight to safeguard consumer interests.

The power to regulate enhances the ability of the government to achieve its service delivery objectives in an economically sustainable way. After it allows for the privatization of a service, the government can regulate tariffs and the returns private firms can earn on their investment. The regulation of tariff increases protects consumers and regulation on returns/profits puts the government in a position to earn any excess profits (above levels that private firms require as fair compensation for their invested capital and effort). When a firm fails to meet service-delivery standards, the government reserves the right to terminate the contract and reallocate it to other providers. In its capacity as a regulator of service providers, the government is in a strong position to create incentives for private operators to deliver services that are better aligned to consumer interests.

8

THE VALUE OF MONEY
RISKS ARISING
FROM THE GOVERNMENT'S MONOPOLY OVER
MONEY-SUPPLY

What a sound money system does is to stabilize all the elements in it, and reduces the uncertainty that people confront. And the one thing all human beings do when they are confronted with uncertainty is pull back, withdraw, disengage, and that means economic activity, which is really dealing with people, just goes straight down.
—Alan Greenspan, Chairman of the U.S. Federal Reserve from 1987 to 2006.

What is the value of money? Does having more money make one wealthy? The quest for riches or wealth is always associated with having more money. However, wealth may be more accurately determined by the purchasing power for goods and services rather than the amount of money a person has. Having more money does not by itself guarantee higher levels of affordability. Furthermore, when prices are not stable, the connection between the quantity of money a person has and his purchasing power or wealth can break down.

An example to illustrate the superiority of purchasing power over absolute income levels in determining standards of living. Teachers from six countries (see fig. 8.1) were polled to estimate the level of affordability that their wages could command in major cities of their respective countries. For the purpose of this exercise, we use the same consumption basket across all countries and assume that every teacher consumes four main items: housing, food, transportation, and entertainment. We also standardize items in the consumption basket to ensure that they are comparable. For example, in order to compare rental costs, apartments or houses have to be located in a major city and offer a comparable living space.

In this simplified and theoretical example, data on teacher incomes and the cost of living in major cities within their respective countries illustrates that earning more money may not always translate into stronger purchasing power or higher living standards. The Indian teacher commands the highest purchasing power in his city. His monthly income can afford to purchase 130% of his consumption basket, even though he only earns a monthly salary of $300. His purchasing power exceeds that of his US counterpart, who earns much higher wages but can barely afford to live in a major city. In order to make ends meet, the American teacher may be forced to downsize her housing unit and reduce her food and entertainment consumption. Even though the American teacher earns more money, her purchasing power is lower and she may feel poorer than the teacher from India. In order to afford the same purchasing power as the teacher from India, the American teacher needs an income of $3400 per month (i.e. to purchase 130% of her consumption basket in the United States).

Figure 8.1. Money vs. Purchasing Power (affordability).

Comparing the Purchasing Power of Teacher Salaries Across Six Countries

Country	Monthly Teacher Income (US$)	Rent ($)	Food ($)	transport ation ($)	entertain ment ($)	cost of consumption basket ($)	Purchasing power of monthly income i.e. proportion of consumption basket that monthly income can buy	Ranking of affordability levels
India	300	100	70	50	10	230	130%	1
Japan	2,000	1300	300	200	100	1,900	105%	3
Mali	100	40	45	10	5	100	100%	5
Mexico	800	450	200	200	50	900	89%	6
Spain	1,500	700	250	200	100	1,250	120%	2
United Kingdom	2,400	1500	350	300	200	2,350	102%	4
USA	2,200	1600	500	300	200	2,600	85%	7

Source: Author

THE HISTORY OF MONEY

Every person, no matter how talented, derives great value from having the ability to obtain goods produced by others in exchange for his production or income. The most important function of money is to serve as a widely accepted medium of exchange to facilitate transactions. Throughout history, various instruments (forms of money) have been employed to facilitate exchange. Once established as a medium of exchange, money can become useful in serving as a store of value (a means to save) and provides a means to account for the value of goods, income or wealth.

Money is any instrument that can be exchanged for a wide variety of goods and services.

Barter. Before the invention and use of money, goods were exchanged more directly (barter). For example, in order to improve the well-being of each party, a potato grower will exchange some potatoes for meat from a shepherd. The barter system was useful in improving people's welfare, but it was not a convenient mechanism for facilitating exchange. Under this system, an exchange can only occur when the needs or wants of the two parties involved happen to match. If the shepherd prefers corn to potatoes, a potato farmer who is still interested in consuming meat has no direct way of exchanging potatoes for meat and must first find a corn producer who will be interested in exchanging corn for potatoes. If he is unable to find a suitable partner to exchange potatoes for corn, the potato farmer's quest for meat, even though he can afford it, may go unfulfilled.

Agricultural commodity money. Agricultural commodities were the first broadly accepted forms of money. Money is any instrument that can be exchanged for a wide variety of goods and services. In order to resolve the matching problem under the barter system, a few valuable commodities such as cows, oxen, bushels of corn, and so forth, were adopted as mediums of exchange (money) to facilitate trade. With a widely accepted medium of exchange, the potato grower in the previous example could exchange (sell) a potato harvest for a number of cows or bushels of corn, which will provide a means to directly purchase any item of his desire, so long as he can afford it. By serving *as a widely accepted medium of exchange*, agricultural commodities such as cows or corn created value for society beyond their intrinsic nutritional value. People with no interest in raising cows or growing corn made extensive use of these items as a medium to facilitate exchange.

Once a widely accepted medium of exchange has been established, it also becomes useful for assessing the value of goods and accounting for wealth or income. People can now more accurately account for their wealth in terms of the number of cows or bushels of corn that they own or can purchase with their assets or income. Artisans can now assess the value of their production in units of money (the number of cows or bushels of corn) and make more informed decisions about how to price or value their work. As a widely recognized and understandable measure of value, money helps people to make more informed decisions about how they employ their resources for production, investment, or consumption.

Agricultural commodities facilitated the exchange of goods and helped to assess value, but they have two key limitations: They are not easily divisible and are not storable for long periods. If people who own cows want to buy salt, they may be forced to exchange their cows for an enormous quantity of salt, beyond their needs. Cows and corn are not convenient to store. It is costly to keep cows. One has to feed them at some cost, and they can also die from disease or old age. Corn may rot and can be destroyed by pests. The high cost of storing agricultural commodities reduces the ability of people to save (store money) over long periods to fund large investments.

Metal Money. The introduction of metal money (e.g., gold and silver) helped to resolve the limitations of agricultural commodity money and facilitated more transactions. Metals are storable for very long periods. There are other avenues to store value, for example, by purchasing real estate and other durable goods. However, when excess income in stored in the form of money (a widely accepted medium of exchange), it increases the ease with which one can make use of stored wealth. For money to retain value, its supply has to be limited. Gold, silver, and other metals were used as money because they were limited in supply, easy to store, and divisible into smaller weights or units. The divisibility of money (in this case metals) allows for a higher range of transactions.

For money to retain value, its supply has to be limited.

In order to perform its functions effectively, the value of money has to be verifiable and stable over time. To maintain its usefulness as a widely accepted medium of exchange, a basis for measuring value and a reliable means to save, money has to be readily verifiable and maintain its value over time. Agricultural commodities were broadly accepted and used as money because they were readily verifiable and kept their value. There is no doubt in people's minds about what a cow looks like or what it may be worth. A cow has an intrinsic value in nutrition and is actively traded in many markets. It is not possible to adulterate or fictitiously cheapen the composition of a cow in order to obtain more money for the same cow. The value of a precious metal is determined by its weight and its purity. Authenticating the purity of metal money may be more challenging. Precious metals can be easily combined with other metals of lower value. In an attempt to make money illegally for themselves, people were tempted to blend lower-value metals into precious metals in order to fraudulently increase the overall weight or value. In order to protect themselves from such fraudulent abuses, people always needed to weigh and verify the purity (a more challenging task) of metals before transactions could be completed. This constant requirement for verification, introduced an inconvenience that restricted exchange.

For the purpose of promoting public trust in metal money and preserving its usefulness as a medium of exchange, governments stepped in, to "guarantee" or certify the purity and weight (hence the value) of metal money with an official stamp. The government took over the supply of money and used its official seal to back the purity and weight of metal coins. Originally, this public trust was fully backed by the appropriate quantity and purity of precious metals in coins. For example, the British pound sterling or the French livre (used from the 8th to the 18th centuries) originally contained one pound by weight of silver of a known purity. In each case, the government was honestly providing a highly useful certification service, solely in public interest.

Like many other institutions, governments may sometimes have strong incentives to use their influence to serve their own interests at the expense of citizens (or other clients). Governments may have initially taken over the supply of money in order to restore public trust, but some will go on to legally abuse their monopoly positions over money supply to defraud their citizens to great extents by arbitrarily diluting the quantity of gold or silver contained in metal money or printing large quantities of new paper money to dilute its value.

In an effort to facilitate trade across distant regions and between countries, paper forms of money were developed to provide more convenient ways to transport money. Banks and reputable merchants wrote letters of credit that were backed by gold or silver and redeemable at bank branches. The general acceptance of letters of credit as money, encouraged governments to issue paper money. Originally, the banknotes issued by governments were backed by metal commodities and were theoretically convertible into gold or silver coins. However, the metal backing was removed over time. Unlike agricultural-commodity money or metal money, paper money is not backed by any real goods of substance. The use of paper money increases the extent to which a government's monopoly over money supply can be abused at the expense of its citizens. The value of money today, its usefulness for transactions, and its ability to serve as a reliable means to store wealth and a basis for measuring value are solely dependent on the integrity of the issuing government or central bank. In countries that manage the value of money with integrity, higher levels of public trust and credibility in money retaining its value creates greater potential for economic transactions, savings, and long-term investment

The use of paper money increases the extent to which a government's monopoly over money supply can be abused at the expense of its citizens. The value of paper money is solely dependent on the credibility of the issuing government.

The quest for more convenient, safe, and reliable mediums of exchange continues. In many countries, bank cards are now more widely used for transactions than currency bills and coins. Supported by advances in online security, various forms of online payment tools are now being adopted due to their superior convenience.

THE GOVERNMENT IS RESPONSIBLE FOR MANAGING THE VALUE OF MONEY AND ENSURING PRICE STABILITY

Sustained periods of high price increases occur when the government abuses its monopoly over money supply to finance its spending plans. Sustained periods of high price increases typically occur when the value of money that people hold, save, or earn is eroded for the benefit of the government. Erosion in the value of money means that each unit of currency buys fewer goods or that one needs more money to buy the same item (i.e., prices rise).

The inflation rate helps to quantify the rate at which prices of goods have increased over a given period or the degree to which the value of money has been eroded. On any given day, prices of some goods may rise, prices of others may fall, and some remain unchanged in price. Price fluctuations in individual goods are not a major concern because they may offset one another and are unlikely to result in a material erosion in purchasing power. When prices rise across a broad spectrum of goods in the economy, households may become poorer, because rising prices reduce affordability levels. When a person's income or a given amount of money is no longer able to purchase his typical consumption basket or can only buy a smaller proportion of items, it means his income or money (which may even go up in quantity) has lost value and the consumer has suffered a loss of purchasing power or affordability.

Sustained periods of high price increases (high rates of erosion in the value of money)

typically arise when the government prints too much money. Like any other commodity, the supply of money is instrumental in determining its value. When the government prints a considerable amount of money to finance its spending needs, the amount of money in the economy increases faster than the amount of goods produced. The far greater availability of money compared to goods produced drive up the price of each good.

For money to retain value, its supply has to be limited.

We typically describe these circumstances as ones in which prices are going up, but it may be more accurate to say that the value of money has been eroded (by government action). The more accurate description makes is easier for people to recognize the source of the problem. The government's ability to create money from thin air, at its discretion, would not be possible if currencies were backed by and readily redeemable for real goods of defined quantity and verifiable quality (e.g., gold and silver of known purity). Banknotes and money backed by credit cards and the like have no intrinsic value.

Which statement on inflation is most common versus potentially more informative?

1. Prices of goods have gone up by 50 percent this year.

2. The government (or central bank) has eroded the value of the money by 33 percent this year? This is an additional tax that people were not aware of.

Statement 1 is most common and statement 2 is potentially more informative.

A 50 percent price increase corresponds to a 33 percent erosion in the value of money. With a 50 percent price increase over a year, an item that sold for 1 unit of currency last year will sell for 1.5 units this year. In the current year, each unit of currency will be able to buy only two-thirds of what it could have bought in the prior year. Hence, the currency (i.e., money) has lost a third of its value.

*****

HIGH INFLATION IS A GOVERNMENT TAX BY STEALTH.

Sustained periods of high price increases lead to a loss of purchasing power for most private citizens. The loss is a direct result of a government tax by stealth on all citizens who use the national currency. We experience sustained periods of high price increases when the government prints large quantities of money to finance its spending needs. In order to earn money to finance their spending needs, citizens and businesses need to labour in the production of goods and services. The honest way for the government to earn money, is to take a share of the income that citizens and businesses generate through the production of real goods and services. However, with its monopoly over money supply, the government also has the ability to legally abuse public trust by creating money for its own use out of thin air, i.e., money that is not backed by the production of real goods. When the government dilutes the value of money for its benefit, it does so at the expense of private citizens and businesses who suffer losses in their levels of affordability. By printing large quantities of new notes to dilute the value of money in the economy, the government extracts value from citizens by stealth.

The ability to control money supply can be used responsibly to stabilize the economy through cycles and to temporarily stimulate the economy in times of great uncertainty. When power over money supply is used responsibly, money retains its value and prices remain stable. However, the power over money supply can be easily abused to serve the government's own interest at the expense of its citizens. Excessive money printing erodes the value of money and drives up prices of all goods in the economy. In an environment of high price increases, income and wealth received or stored in money (as opposed to real goods) lose value. This is a tax on all citizens who hold or make transactions with the national currency.

Paper money (banknotes or bills) has no intrinsic value; it cannot be consumed directly, and needs to be exchanged for real goods. Paper money only has value to the extent that people are willing to accept it in exchange for goods. If people were to lose complete confidence in money, the government's monopoly over money supply would become worthless. There are several examples in history, of citizens losing complete trust in their national currencies and resorting to alternative forms of exchange, including the use of commodity money and barter. When the government prints large quantities of money, it is not creating real wealth in the economy. The government is simply transferring a proportion of the value of goods produced by citizens to itself in an irresponsible manner that catches citizens off-guard. The government takes a proportion of the income and wealth of citizens without their consent or knowledge. This can be regarded as theft but one that is legal. Still, the legality of this theft does not make it an appropriate course of action for a government and does not change the fact that it is a clear abuse of public trust.

Taking resources from citizens without their consent or knowledge is not a responsible way to collect taxes. Payers of this tax are not aware of their tax bill; they do not know how much they are paying currently or how much they might eventually pay. The tax is extracted slowly as the government prints money, and the erosion in purchasing power suffered by citizens builds up over time. The situation is analogous to an undercover scheme to leak pennies from one's wallet every second or minute. It is only over time that one realizes that his purchasing power has been meaningfully eroded. However, even after one realizes the loss of affordability, the source of the loss may still not be clear.

The government's monopoly over printing money is essentially a blank cheque that citizens have handed over to their government. The cheque can be drawn against their income and savings at any time. The government's monopoly over money supply has been abused, at some point, in the history of almost all countries. The broad historical experience of this abuse in almost all countries should encourage all citizens to actively monitor their governments to ensure integrity in the management of monetary affairs. If a government is managing its currency with integrity today, it cannot be taken for granted that this will continue into perpetuity.

Figure 8.2. Inflation and Money Supply Growth (2008–2013)

Countries with high rates of money-supply growth have high inflation rates

Highest Inflation countries in the world	Average Annual Money Supply growth	Average Annual Inflation (price increase)	Price increases over the 5 year period	Erosion in the Value of money over the period
Venezuela, RB	48%	35%	355%	-78%
Belarus	51%	32%	303%	-75%
Sudan	27%	27%	232%	-70%
Guinea	29%	17%	124%	-55%
Sao Tome and Prin.	23%	17%	117%	-54%
Sierra Leone	30%	16%	112%	-53%
Malawi	43%	16%	110%	-52%
Pakistan	16%	16%	106%	-51%
Burundi	21%	15%	105%	-51%
Ghana	36%	15%	104%	-51%
Mongolia	32%	15%	101%	-50%
Angola	34%	15%	99%	-50%
Vietnam	27%	15%	98%	-49%
Nigeria	21%	14%	91%	-48%
Egypt, Arab Rep.	14%	14%	90%	-47%

Countries with low rates of money-supply growth have low inflation rates

Lowest Inflation countries in the world	Average Annual Money Supply growth	Average Annual Inflation (price increase)	Price increases over the 5 year period	Erosion in the Value of money over the period
Sweden	2.3%	1.6%	8%	-7%
France	4.9%	1.9%	10%	-9%
Chile	9.3%	1.9%	10%	-9%
Germany	0.1%	1.9%	10%	-9%
Morocco	8.3%	2.0%	10%	-9%
Portugal	8.3%	2.0%	10%	-9%
Canada	2.8%	2.0%	10%	-9%
United States	5.2%	2.4%	12%	-11%
Netherlands	4.2%	2.5%	13%	-11%
Norway	0.0%	2.5%	13%	-12%
Italy	7.6%	2.5%	13%	-12%
Finland	6.9%	2.6%	14%	-12%
Denmark	2.3%	2.6%	14%	-12%
Austria	1.4%	2.7%	14%	-12%
Bahamas	2.4%	2.7%	14%	-12%
Belgium	4.7%	2.8%	15%	-13%

Source: Author, IMF

A history of high inflation can be costly to correct. Citizens often use their experience of price increases to set expectations for wages and prices in the future. The anchoring of future prices on inflation expectations mutes the impact of central-bank action to restore price stability in the short to medium term. Restoring price stability after a period of high inflation may only be possible by raising interest rates to punitive levels and taking other measures that restrict economic growth for a sustained period.

Rate of price increases (inflation) ≈ degree to which the government has eroded the value of money ≈ rate of government tax by stealth or the size of its inflation tax.

Adam Smith (Father of Modern Economics), **on the History of Governments and Money**

"For in every country of the world, I believe the avarice and injustices of sovereign states abusing the confidence of their subjects have by degrees diminished the real quantity of metal which has been originally contained in their coins *(i.e., eroding the value of money)*. The Roman As or Pondo *(pound)* in the latter ages of the republic, was reduced to twenty-fourth part of its original value and instead of weighing a pound, came to weigh only half an ounce. The English pound and penny contain at present about a third only, the Scots pound and penny about a thirty-sixth and the French pound and penny about a sixty-sixth part of their original value. By means of these operations, the princes and sovereigns who performed them were enabled in appearance to pay their debts and to fulfil their engagement with smaller quantities of silver than would otherwise have been requisite. It was indeed in appearance only for the creditors were really defrauded of a part of what was due them. All other debtors in the state were allowed the same privilege and might pay with the same nominal sum of the new and debased coin whatever they had borrowed in the old. Such operations have therefore always proved favourable to the debtor and ruinous to the creditor *(in a broader sense, anyone who depends on the state or others for a payment)* and have sometimes produced a greater and more universal revolution in the fortunes of private persons, than could have been occasioned by a very great public calamity." (Source: The Wealth of Nations, 1776).

How the rate of price increases in the economy (the inflation rate) is measured.
Consumer inflation is the most broadly used measure of price increases in the economy. Consumer inflation is measured by comparing prices in a standardized basket of goods and services that are bought by the typical consumer, such as rent, food, transportation, entertainment, and other items. Each of the subgroups is assigned a relevant weight based on its importance in the consumer basket, and each subgroup includes specific

consumer items and their prices. For example, under the food subgroup, there will be prices for specified quantities of milk, eggs, bread, and other foods consumed by the typical household in the country. Consumer inflation is assessed by taking a monthly survey of prices for each of the items in the basket. These prices are multiplied by their respective weights to obtain aggregate information about price levels in the economy. The inflation figure is obtained by comparing changes in aggregate price levels over a month, a year, or any other relevant period. The inflation measure provides information about the rate of price increases in the economy over a given period. This information also reflects the extent to which the value of money or its purchasing power has been eroded.

*****

High levels of price increases can create alarming compounded effects over time. At extreme levels, excessive money printing by the government can wipe out public trust in a currency as a reliable medium of exchange. Due to the compounding effect of price increases, high levels of inflation can have a material negative impact on economic incentives and economic growth. An environment of stable prices enables households and businesses to make more informed consumption choices and save towards future investments. In countries with high levels of inflation, the ability to plan for the future is highly restricted because prices go out of control over the long term. For example, with annual price increases of 2%, the price of a typical product is likely to increase by 10% in five years and by 22% percent in ten years. If a person plans to finance a medium-term investment with regular (e.g., monthly) savings of a fixed amount of money, the total savings would be close enough to the true cost of the investment in five or 10 years, when inflation rates are low and stable. On the other hand, in a country that has annual price increases of 20%, the price of a typical product will increase by 150% in five years and by 500% in ten years. When prices of goods in an economy increase by over 500% in ten years, this means that the currency in the economy has lost over 80% of its value in the period. With a 500% price increase, an item that was priced at one unit of currency ten years ago is likely to command a price of 6 currency units today. Over this period, the currency would have lost 84% of its value because one unit of currency can now afford about one-sixth (or 16%) of the same product it was able to buy ten years ago. A high level of uncertainty about future prices erodes the incentive to save, distorts the allocation of economic resources, and restricts economic growth.

In some countries, one has to spend hundreds, thousands, or millions of units of the national currency to buy basic items such as bread. The amount of money required to buy these basic items can increase materially in a person's lifetime. High and rising currency denominations (i.e., the number of units of currency that appear on bills and coins) represent the compounded effect of policies that have eroded the value of money over time. Money can lose so much value over time that governments in these countries sometimes simply wipe out several zeros from currency bills to reset the clock. For example, in January 2005, the Turkish central bank issued new currency bills that wiped out six zeros from the old bill. One new Turkish lira had the same value as 1,000,000 old Turkish lira. In 2007, the government of Ghana issued a new currency that wiped out four zeros from the old one. One new Ghana cedi was equivalent in value to 10,000 units of the old cedi. The use of money supply growth to stimulate economic activity remains a key part of government policy in Ghana and Turkey. As a result of high inflation rates, these new currencies have already lost significant value since they were issued. Basic goods that were priced at one unit of currency when the new bills were first introduced were selling for two to three units of currency by 2014. In the course of a decade, the new currencies have lost 30% to 50% of their value.

Figure 8.3. Connecting the inflation rate to the rate of erosion in the value of money. Calculated examples

Cumulative Price Increase After					
Annual Inflation rate (annual price increase)	1 year	2 years	3 years	5 years	10 years
2%	2%	4%	6%	10%	22%
5%	5%	10%	16%	28%	63%
10%	10%	21%	33%	61%	159%
15%	15%	32%	52%	101%	305%
20%	20%	44%	73%	149%	519%
30%	30%	69%	120%	271%	1279%
50%	50%	125%	238%	659%	5667%

Cumulative Erosion in Value of Money After					
Annual Inflation rate (annual price increase)	1 year	2 years	3 years	5 years	10 years
2%	2%	4%	6%	9%	18%
5%	5%	9%	14%	22%	39%
10%	9%	17%	28%	38%	61%
15%	13%	24%	34%	50%	75%
20%	17%	31%	42%	60%	84%
30%	23%	41%	54%	73%	93%
50%	33%	56%	70%	87%	98%

Source: Author

MONEY ILLUSION

In sustained periods of high price increases (high inflation), money becomes a less reliable measure of value or unit of account and has a tendency to create illusions of gain. Money serves a key function in helping us measure or account for the value of goods, income, and wealth. When prices are stable, money becomes a reliable measure of value, and an increase in the amount of money earned reflect a fundamental increase in purchasing power. However, in sustained periods of high price increases, the value of money is eroded so rapidly that large increases in the quantity of money that a person earns may not necessarily increase his purchasing power. Money becomes a less reliable measure of value or unit of account under periods of high price increases. Money has a tendency to create illusions of wealth in periods of high price increases. In order to understand the fundamental value of money, it is important to distinguish between **nominal variables** (accounted for in units of money) and **real variables**. Real variables correct for the risk of illusion in money by expressing the value of money in terms of its purchasing power for goods and services (i.e., real items with intrinsic value). A real variable adjusts for the illusionary effect of money and represents the true or fundamental value of income, profits, or wealth. Real variables are therefore more reliable for making economic decisions. The **real change** in income levels (i.e., the change in the purchasing power of income) corrects for the illusionary effect of inflation on income. The *real change* in wages (or in any other variable) can be estimated by subtracting the inflation rate from the percentage change in nominal wages (or percentage change in the variable).

Money serves as a reliable measure of value only when prices are stable.

Real goods have an intrinsic value in consumption or use. Increases in the supply of real goods (e.g., food, clothing or housing) improve living standards of people, because an increase in supply is likely to make these goods more affordable. Paper money has no intrinsic value. We cannot consume paper money directly. We exchange it for goods and services that have an intrinsic value. Paper money only has value when the general public is willing to accept it in exchange for goods and services. Exchanging paper money for real goods is only possible because of the trust the general public has in the issuing government. When the value of paper money is rapidly eroded, the general public can lose confidence in the currency as a reliable medium of exchange. In extreme cases, people can abandon the use of their national currency for trade and resort to less convenient or more primitive mechanisms for trade. For example, in countries that experience high levels of inflation, a significant number of transactions are priced in foreign currencies that have a better history of price stability. In countries that experience extreme levels of inflation or hyperinflation, people may resort to barter or use various commodities and other real goods for exchange. Real goods have an intrinsic value that is supported by other real goods (such as labour and raw materials) employed in their production. The fundamental value of real goods is therefore less susceptible to the illusionary effect of money or policies that erode the value of money.

Real variables correct for the illusionary effects of inflation and are most relevant for making economic decisions.

Due to poor levels of financial literacy, many people measure the value of money in nominal terms and may be at risk of falling victim to money illusion. Many people tend to evaluate their wages and wealth in nominal terms, that is, in the observable amount of money they earn or have. When people focus on observable amounts of money earned or owned, their ability to assess changes in their purchasing power in response to changes in price levels may be compromised. Money illusion occurs when large increases in income do not correspond to increases in purchasing power. The risk of this illusion increases in sustained periods of high price increases (an environment of high inflation). Real analysis of income, wages, profits, revenue growth, and other economic variables is always useful but becomes absolutely necessary during periods of high price increases. Analyzing information in real terms is important because real variable are more representative of changes in purchasing power and living standards. Increases in wages, income, pensions and wealth are most relevant not in their absolute nominal terms but in the way they affect affordability (i.e., purchasing power) for goods and services.

Generally, in periods of low and stable inflation (price increases of 0–5% over the course of a year), real adjustments become less necessary over short periods of time. When the inflation rate is low and stable, nominal (or observed) changes in income are more likely to be closely linked with changes in purchasing power. Real analysis becomes most relevant in periods of high price changes. High levels of price increases necessitate real adjustments on a more frequent basis, such as annually or quarterly. In extreme cases of inflation, monthly, weekly, or even daily adjustments may be necessary.

Nominal vs. Real Analysis—Worked Example 1

In nominal terms, an employee's wages went up from $1,000 per month in the first year of employment to $1,500 per month in his second year. Did he achieve a 50% increase in affordability? Is the 50% increase in wages **real?** In the third year, the employee continued to work equally hard, but due to weak economic conditions and poor corporate sales and profits (of his employer) his wages were cut from $1,500 to $1,400 per month. How bad is the 7% wage cut? Is this a **real** loss of purchasing power? How does the employee feel about it?

Real analysis assesses the value of money in terms of its purchasing power for goods and services. For the purpose of simplifying real analysis, let us assume that this worker spends all his monthly income on a basket of two goods only: rent and 25 kilos of potatoes each month. Furthermore, let us assume that the cost of the monthly rent increased to $800 in year two from $500 in year one (a 60% increase) and the price of a kilogram of potatoes increased from $4 to $7 (a 75% increase). Based on the analysis below, *we can conclude that his wage increase in the second year was not real, it was only an illusion of gain.* His affordability for real goods (rent and potatoes) actually fell by 23% because the price of his consumption basket rose faster than his wages. In year three, due to poorer conditions in the overall economy, his wages were reduced by 7% to $1400 a month. However, the same economic weakness that resulted in his wage cut also triggered a lower demand for goods and caused prices of most products in the economy to fall. His wages fell by 7% but rent and potato prices fell by much more (13 and 14% respectively). The purchasing power associated with his wage was therefore higher in year three (as compared to year two) even though the amount of money he got paid in wages was reduced.

Wages and prices of consumer goods ($)	Year 1	Year 2	Year 3
Price of Potatoes/Kg	4	7	6
Rent	500	800	700
Wages	1000	1500	1400
Rate of price increases (inflation)			
Potatoes		75%	-14%
Rent		60%	-13%
Wages		50%	-7%
Price of monthly consumption basket			
(rent + price of 25 kilos of potatoes)	600	975	850
Purchasing power of monthly wage			
(number of baskets that a monthly wage			
can afford)	1.67	1.54	1.65
Changes in wealth			
Nominal (wage increase/decrease)		50%	-7%
Real (increase or decrease in			
affordability for the consumption basket)		-8%	7%

Workers should focus on changes in real wages not on nominal wage increases.
Workers everywhere in the world have an objective to increase their earning power in order to improve their living standards. However, obsession with large wage increases rather than gains in purchasing power may ultimately support high inflation policies. When prices of goods in the economy are rising fast, workers may succeed in bargaining for sizeable wage increases but may experience an erosion in their purchasing power, because prices of goods may increase at a faster rate than wages. In order to correct for the effects of money illusion, workers should negotiate to maintain or improve their real wages rather than focus primarily on increasing the amount of money they take home in salary.

In periods of unfavourable economic conditions, weak government finances may mean that the wages of public sector employees may have to be cut or frozen. Private sector employees may also face the prospects of wage cuts under unfavorable economic conditions. Being honest about economic challenges and the need to undertake difficult decisions on wages and spending plans may be more rewarding over the long term than pursuing an illusionary policy of raising wages and stimulating the economy through the printing of large amounts of money. The honest approach provides citizens and businesses with accurate information about economic challenges and the need for austerity in spending habits. On the other hand, the illusionary effect of a monetary stimulus, while providing misleading comfort to employees in the short term, may ultimately ruin their economic prospects by depleting their purchasing power.

When the government chooses to finance unaffordable spending plans by printing money, it is essentially imposing a hidden tax on its citizens. Citizens are likely to suffer an erosion in their purchasing power or living standards over time, even if they receive wage increases through the period. When the government creates an illusion of wealth under challenging economic conditions by printing money and raising the level of wages, it is simply playing on the ignorance of citizens about how the value of paper money is determined. When citizens are better informed about the power of the government to use its money printing monopoly to wipe out large proportions of their purchasing power, they may be less willing to cooperate with inflation policies. With a broader understanding of the ability of the government to create money from thin air, often at the expense of citizens and businesses, workers are more likely to focus on real changes in wage conditions rather than nominal increases.

When the government does not manage money supply to ensure price stability, wage increases may not correspond to gains in purchasing power.

In the economic history of some countries, erosion in the value of money has been so painful that labour unions and employees now embed inflation expectations in their wage negotiations, and strong unions try to link annual wage increases to inflation rates to protect their purchasing power in real terms. Extreme inflation developments in the history of some countries have created strong public knowledge about their ill effects for average citizens, who have awoken to their rightful role, to monitor government action and spur better governance. When inflation rates set the floor for wage negotiations, governments may be less likely to pursue high inflation policies. In countries like Brazil, as a result of democratized watchfulness over inflation, elected governments have become more responsible in supporting a stable monetary regime, and they see the risk of rising inflation as one of the most potent risks to maintaining political support.

Nominal vs. Real Analysis—Worked Example 2

Erosion in the purchasing power of wages in an environment of sustained price increases. The average annual wage for public sector employees in a country was 12,000 units of the national currency. A typical public sector employee spends his wages on rent, food, transportation and entertainment. At the beginning of the period, the average public sector employee is spent 10,000 on his consumption basket and had extra income (2,000) for savings and other activities. For the following decade, the government pursues a high inflation policy which leads to prices of basic goods rising by 20% every year. Public sector employees demand higher wages to compensate for the high price increases in the economy and the government eventually approves 10% annual wage increases for all public sector employees. Because the rate of prices increases in the economy (i.e. the inflation rate) is higher than public sector wage increases, every year, the purchasing power of public sector employees is eroded. At the beginning of the period, public sector employee wages could afford 120% of the consumption basket. After one year of high inflation, affordability for the consumption basket falls to 110% (a 10% erosion in purchasing power). Even though public sector employees receive a 10% wage increase, after adjusting for the effect of the 20% inflation in the cost of their consumption basket, real wages contracted by 10%. (The approximate annual real adjustment can be obtained by subtracting the annual inflation rate from the annual percentage increase in wages).

When sustained over long periods, high inflation policies have the potential to materially erode the purchasing power of workers. The loss of purchasing power after one year of high inflation is only modest and public sector employees can still afford to purchase their consumption basket. However, over longer periods of time, public sector employees start to feel a strong depletion in their purchasing power. By year three, they can barely afford their consumption basket. After five years, affordability for the consumption basket drops to 78% (compared to 120% at the beginning of the period). After ten years, public sector employee wages can only afford 50% of their initial consumption basket. Because the purchasing power of wages has been materially eroded, public sector employees will be forced to reduce their overall consumption. Even though public sector employees are losing their purchasing power year after year, because they are receiving salary increases, they may initially be under an illusion of gain, however the erosion in purchasing power is so material that eventually they would come to terms with the fact that in real terms, the government has indeed been cutting their salaries year after year. In order to enhance their welfare, all workers (including public sector workers) should aim for wage increases in real terms and where this is not possible, they should try to preserve the purchasing power of wages in real terms (i.e., ask for wage increases that are at least in line with inflation)

	Today	Year 1	Year 2	Year 3	Year 4	Year 5
Annual Salary (growing by 10% p.a.)	**12,000**	**13,200**	**14,520**	**15,972**	**17,569**	**19,326**
Annual Expenditure (growing at 20% inflation rate p.a.)						
Rent	5000	6,000	7,200	8,640	10,368	12,442
Food	3500	4,200	5,040	6,048	7,258	8,709
Transportation	1000	1,200	1,440	1,728	2,074	2,488
Entertainment	500	600	720	864	1,037	1,244
Cost of Consumption Basket	**10,000**	**12,000**	**14,400**	**17,280**	**20,736**	**24,883**
Affordability for consumption basket (income/cost of consumption basket)	**120%**	**110%**	**101%**	**92%**	**85%**	**78%**

Source: Author

IN PERIODS OF HIGH INFLATION, ECONOMIC INDICATORS MAY BE MISLEADING BECAUSE MONEY BECOMES A LESS RELIABLE UNIT OF ACCOUNT OR MEASURE OF VALUE.

In an environment of high price increases, consumers may make drastic changes to their consumption baskets and reported inflation figures based on fixed consumption baskets may no longer be reliable. In their efforts to protect the purchasing power of their income, consumers change the composition of their consumption basket in response to high price increases. For example, consumers may buy fewer units of the most expensive goods and may be forced to stockpile basic necessities. When consumers change their consumption patterns frequently, inflation figures may become less accurate in reflecting price changes in the economy. This is because the reported inflation figures attempt to measure price changes in a basket of goods that is no longer representative of the consumption patterns of a typical household. In countries that pursue inflation policies, interest rates are typically much higher than inflation levels. This means that those who lend to these governments require a higher level of compensation to preserve the purchasing power of money than what is indicated by official inflation figures.

Rising price increases (including wages) under weak economic conditions when real demand for goods is low and unemployment levels are rising can only be an

illusion created by poor money management practices. When money is managed with integrity, price changes are better correlated with changes in underlying demand and employment conditions. In periods of strong economic growth and growing employment opportunities, the rate of inflation tends to increase to reflect the improvement in demand conditions. On the other hand, in periods of low demand and rising unemployment prices rise at a slower rate. When money is managed with integrity, the positive correlation between inflation rates and the economic cycle is more intuitive. It is more reasonable to expect businesses to increase prices in periods of strong demand.

In countries where money is not managed with integrity, the link between price and value can break down. For example, durable goods such as cars are supposed to fall in value as they age because they become less reliable over time. However, in countries where there is no commitment to price stability, the price of durable goods such as cars can increase as they age. This creates illusions of gain on assets that are undergoing a depletion in fundamental value.

In countries where money is not managed with integrity, the link between price and value can break down.

In periods of high inflation, any form of accounting for households and businesses may become less meaningful because money may no longer be a reliable unit of account. For example, in an environment of sustained high inflation, many businesses may automatically be posting strong revenue and profit growth, and many employees will be receiving high wage increases. This observation appears to indicate improving prospects for businesses and households. However, in most cases, the growth in profits or wages turns out to be an illusion. Business prospects and living conditions are more likely to decline rather than improve under periods of high price increases. In such periods, a business can increase profits even when the actual volume of business in terms of units of products sold is declining. Because prices of all goods have risen sharply, the increase in revenue and business profits may not be enough to fund the restocking of products that have been sold. This means, that while profits may be superficially increasing, the underlying business may be shrinking in value.

In countries with high levels of inflation, consumer behaviour may not always be intuitive (even though it may be reasonable). In such countries, prices tend to rise at a faster pace when demand conditions are worsening. Consumers may accelerate the purchase of durable goods (cars, houses, refrigerators, etc.) at the beginning of an economic downturn. This consumer behaviour is clearly not an expression of confidence in an economic recovery but rather a panic buying of real goods to protect (or hide) incomes and savings from a government inflation tax, which tends to increase under such conditions. In countries where prices are stable, high levels of economic uncertainty reduce demand for durable goods, which is a more intuitive reaction.

 In countries that pursue high inflation policies, interest rates tend to peak when demand for spending and investment is weakest. This is another observation that is not intuitive but explained by government policy that is aimed at depriving citizens of funds and opportunities when they are most in need. When a government is committed to price stability, interest rates rise under favourable economic conditions when spending, investment, and employment levels are booming. When demand and employment levels weaken, interest rates fall to help stimulate the economy.

High inflation alters economic incentives and changes production patterns such that estimates of economic growth based on previous production baskets may no longer be reliable. In some cases it is possible for countries to post **real** (i.e., inflation adjusted) economic growth figures while living standards are falling. The economy may be growing according to official reports but when assessed in terms of more stable foreign currencies, economic output may have materially declined. For example, in recent years living standards in Venezuela have fallen for most people. Basic goods have become unaffordable and, in a number of cases, unavailable. Productivity in the economy has suffered as factories close due to an inability to secure essential supplies. Yet Venezuelan authorities have reported decent real economic growth figures through the period and are forecasting modest growth for the near future. Venezuela is a clear case of an economy suffering from excessive government intervention, weak government finances, and high inflation. However, reported economic variables are not reflecting the sharp decline in living standards that most Venezuelans may have suffered. The disparity may be due to distortions in consumption and production patterns that occurs during periods of high inflation. In many countries that pursue high inflation policies, citizens may not place much value on reported economic growth numbers because they may have lived through several "official economic growth" periods in which they suffered sharp losses in purchasing power.

When money is not managed for price stability, it becomes a less reliable measure of value or basis for accounting. Economic indicators such as the level of economic growth, growth in wages and business profits and growth in investment are only useful for policy makers, business owners, and households when these indicators carry relevant information about changes in living standards and fundamental business prospects. When economic indicators become unreliable, they may further distort policies and economic decisions. Inflation has the potential to create an illusion of gain and lead to a misallocation of resources. The extent of the illusion increases with the rate of inflation. At high levels of inflation, many forms of accounting on the basis of money including business profits, wages growth, and economic growth, may become unreliable, and the "inflation" adjustment may no longer be accurate (because the underlying inflation number becomes less representative of the true level of price increases in the economy).

ECONOMIC CONSEQUENCES OF HIGH INFLATION POLICIES

Living standards of citizens are depressed under sustained periods of high price increases. Periods of high price increases tend to make people poorer, even when they are receiving wage increases. When the government pursues policies that lead to sustained periods of high price increases, it is essentially imposing a tax on its citizens without their knowledge. This slow building tax can depress the purchasing power of citizens over time and lower their quality of life. High levels of inflation may also worsen income inequality in a society, because some wages may adjust faster than others and some firms may have a stronger ability to pass on price increases than others. Unless they are underpinned by productivity gains in the economy, general wage increases are less likely to translate into a sustainable improvement in the purchasing power of workers.

In periods of high price increases, people have strong incentives to immediately consume their income and savings, because money loses value at a fast pace. People are also less willing to lend in such periods, because there is great uncertainty over whether the money they lend out will retain its purchasing power in the future. When the value of money is being eroded by government action, people who hold money for long periods pay the highest penalty (i.e., the highest inflation tax). High inflation tax increases pressure on people to immediately convert income into consumption goods or lose their affordability. High rates of price increases raise incentives for people to channel excess income or savings into durable goods such as property or cars, which keep their value better than money. When the government erodes the value of money, it distorts economic incentives for private citizens and businesses. People buy durable goods or real estate primarily as a means to protect themselves against the government's inflation tax, not because of a belief that these are attractive investments in their own right. Protecting the purchasing power of money becomes the preoccupation of households and businesses, and productive economic activities struggle to attract capital and other resources.

The cost of borrowing rises in periods of high inflation and reduces investment activity. When prices are rising at a fast pace, the government and all other borrowers need to pay high interest rates to compensate lenders for the high risk of eroding the purchasing power of their capital. Furthermore, high levels of immediate consumption reduce the amount of savings available in the economy to finance investment. High levels of interest rates make it more punitive for individuals and companies to finance investments. Firms may also be less likely to invest under such conditions, because pricing for their products may become unpredictable. Firms may face weak demand prospects because the government is depleting the purchasing power (i.e., affordability) of households through its inflation tax.

An environment of high price increases can create economic uncertainty and restrict growth. Prices provide useful information that allows consumers and businesses to allocate resources. When price changes are unpredictable, economic decision making becomes more challenging, and people undertake fewer and less efficient economic actions. When the value of money diminishes rapidly and price increases become unpredictable, firms struggle to set prices for their products. The difficulty in setting prices creates production problems for most businesses, and the overall level of productivity may suffer. For example, a restaurant may have little visibility into what it can charge for meals, because the cost of inputs is unpredictable. Prices of inputs and meals may change at any time. Customers of the restaurant, realizing that they cannot form reasonable expectations of the price of meals, are less likely to patronize the restaurant. High price uncertainty can lead to a loss of sales and profits for the restaurant owners, a loss of jobs for restaurant employees, lower profits and employment opportunities for all other providers of inputs and services for the restaurant, and lower utility for restaurant customers. The relationship between most producers and their customers mirrors that of restaurants and their clients. When prices are not stable, economic activity become restricted.

In periods of high price increases, as people divert their energy into avoiding the inflation tax and adjust to an environment of price uncertainty, more productive segments of the economy struggle to attract attention, and productivity falls. Whatever the initial intentions of a government may be, consistently pursuing policies that erode the value of money ultimately leads to a weak economy, uncertain economic conditions, low purchasing power for households and businesses, weaker government finances, and lower living standards. A vicious cycle is created, because depressed government finances and loss of borrowing credibility under such desperate conditions may force the government to resort to printing more money, which could result in price increases getting out of control.

Integrity Is the Bedrock of Good Governance. Without integrity in managing the value of money, an economy is unlikely to provide and sustain a framework for stability and growth. Historic evidence has shown that integrity can be readily sacrificed for stronger short-term political incentives of elected governments. Citizens have a duty to constantly monitor and demand integrity in the management of government affairs. An objective and observable starting point for good governance is related to providing and maintaining price stability.

TO SERVE THE INTEREST OF CITIZENS, GOVERNMENT POLICY ON MONEY SHOULD HAVE ONE PRIMARY OBJECTIVE: THAT OF MAINTAINING PRICE STABILITY

Central banks or governments can only earn credibility (public trust) on money by delivering a long track record of stable prices. Price stability generally equates to low and stable inflation (modest and predictable price increases in the range of 0-5% per year). Sustaining price stability is a balancing act. Central banks with credibility and a commitment to price stability usually target low levels of inflation (2–3% percent rather than 0%) in order to provide some headroom to respond to economic conditions that might cause a general decline in the prices of goods (deflation). Sustained periods of falling prices (deflation) is associated with falling wages, declining output, high unemployment, and rising indebtedness. Deflationary periods are also less responsive to tools that the central bank can deploy to restore price stability (the primary objective).

To maintain price stability, the level of money supply has to rise in proportion to real growth in the production of goods and services. When money supply growth far exceeds the level of real economic growth, prices are more likely to rise sharply, because the quantity of money available would have risen at a much faster pace than the value of goods produced in the economy. The process of tailoring money supply to the real growth rate in an economy in order to maintain price stability may be simple in principle but challenging to achieve in practice. In addition to economic growth, many other variables (e.g., future price expectations of citizens and businesses) influence price stability. Maintaining price stability through an economic cycle can be a major challenge for central banks. But it is achievable.

Unlike many other economic objectives, price stability is under full government control. In an increasingly interconnected global economy, many economic variables in a given country may not be fully controlled by the government (at least in the short-term), but a government and its central bank have complete control over the issuance and management of the national currency. The national currency in a country is the ultimate property of the government. The government has exclusive rights to print money. The government controls the supply of money and therefore determines the value of each unit of currency. Every government has the ability (but some may not have the willingness) to deliver an environment of stable prices for its economy. All citizens who use any form of government endorsed money are implicitly riding on the credibility of their governments (or central banks) to manage the value of money responsibly.

IF INFLATION IS SO BAD, WHY DO SOME GOVERNMENTS PURSUE INFLATIONARY POLICIES?

Increasing money supply can stimulate the economy over the short-term when prices are stable to begin with. When prices are stable, a short-term increase in the money supply can stimulate economic growth by creating illusions of temporary gain. In the short-term, a number of prices in the economy may be sticky (i.e., may not readily adjust to economic conditions). For example, in periods of economic weakness, prices of many goods and services may fall because of lower demand, however certain prices in the economy like wages and rent do not adjust quickly. The reason is that, employees and homeowners are usually resistant to wage and rent cuts (probably out of fear that once cut, wages and rent will reset and stick to lower levels). Sticky prices such as wages and rent that do not adjust quickly to economic conditions can further depress the level of economic activity in a downturn.

A responsible central bank that has earned the confidence and trust of the public can be effective in stimulating the economy (to reverse the effect of sticky prices) under such dire conditions by temporarily increasing money supply. A modest increase in money supply can stimulate the economy by creating a short term illusion of profits. In the short term, an increase in money supply causes prices of goods and services to rise but wages and other sticky costs may take a while to catch up. Because product prices are rising faster than sticky input costs, profits of businesses may grow and firms may have greater confidence to hire and increase production. Over time, as prices in the economy rise, employees, property owners, and other suppliers of inputs may become aware that their purchasing power has declined in real terms (i.e., that prices have risen faster than their nominal wage or rent increases). Over time, sticky prices and all other prices will adjust to reflect higher price levels in the economy. The effectiveness of the money supply stimulus depends on how fast workers and suppliers of other inputs adjust their expectations for price increases. Once input costs have fully adjusted to inflation expectations, any further monetary stimulus is likely to have a muted impact on economic growth and a more pronounced impact on inflation.

In order to resist strong political incentives to stimulate the economy through money supply, governments in many countries have provided their central banks with strong and independent mandates. True independence of central banks from political influence helps them to become more focused on maintaining price stability and reduces the risk of abusing public trust to finance governments by printing money. The interests of independent central banks and that of private citizens are better aligned.

The ability to use money supply to stimulate economic activity can be exceptionally useful. However it is only effective under central banks and governments that have earned the trust of their citizens in their duty to maintain price stability. The power to use meaningful increases in money supply to stimulate the economy is rarely used by a credible central bank and when employed, the growth in money supply is withdrawn as soon as the economy starts to show signs of recovery or when there is any meaningful risk of inflation rising above targets that are consistent with the objective of maintaining price stability. A credible central bank will never sacrifice its commitment to price stability. It aims instead to restore an economy to "normal levels" of activity by reducing the potential drag of sticky prices in a downturn. A credible central bank will not attempt to create the impression that money-supply increases can be employed to generate sustainable economic growth and gains in living standards.

It is the stability of some prices in the face of economic weakness that drags the economy below its potential. Sticky prices are more likely to be observed under credible central banks that have delivered a long track record of price stability. Some central banks may be independent, but their ability to deliver price stability is compromised by the fact that they may not have a strong track record to earn high levels of public trust. Credibility for price stability goes beyond articles of constitution that support an independent central bank. Credibility is earned by delivering a long track record of price stability. Public trust in price stability helps to embed low and stable inflation expectations for the future.

A money supply economic stimulus is not effective without an anchor of price stability

High levels of political influence over monetary policy increase the risk of money supply being employed as a regular instrument of government financing and stimulus packages. The risk of financing government expenditure by printing money (a stealth tax on all citizens) increases when the economy weakens. The result is that inflation is always high (high single-digit to double-digit annual price increases), and the rate of price increases worsens when the economy weakens.

In countries that pursue high inflation policies, expectations of high price increases are deeply embedded among economic participants. All prices (including wages and rents) are always adjusting upwards. There are no sticky prices. Property owners, employees, and providers of other inputs are accustomed to high rates of price increases and readily incorporate regular upward adjustments in their expectations and price-setting behaviour. The result is that efforts to stimulate the economy with money supply has a limited impact on growth but translates directly into accelerating the rate of price increases. In such countries, the highest rate of price increases is often observed when demand conditions in the economy and government finances are weakest.

HOW THE CENTRAL BANK MANAGES THE VALUE OF MONEY OR PRICE LEVELS IN THE ECONOMY

Money supply refers to the amount of money that is readily accessible for spending in the economy. Money supply consists of currency bills and coins that people hold and accessible bank deposits. Increasing the rate of money supply growth puts upward pressure on prices while decreasing the rate of money supply growth can reduce the rate of inflation. By controlling the level of money supply in an economy, the central bank or the government can control or influence the level of price increases in the economy. Figure 8.2 shows a strong link between the rate of price increases and the growth in money supply.

Figure 8.2. Inflation and Money Supply Growth (2008–2013)

Countries with high rates of money supply growth have high inflation rates.

Highest Inflation countries in the world	Average Annual Money Supply growth	Average Annual Inflation (price increase)	Price increases over the 5 year period	Erosion in the Value of money over the period
Venezuela, RB	48%	35%	355%	-78%
Belarus	51%	32%	303%	-75%
Sudan	27%	27%	232%	-70%
Guinea	29%	17%	124%	-55%
Sao Tome and Prin.	23%	17%	117%	-54%
Sierra Leone	30%	16%	112%	-53%
Malawi	43%	16%	110%	-52%
Pakistan	16%	16%	106%	-51%
Burundi	21%	15%	105%	-51%
Ghana	36%	15%	104%	-51%
Mongolia	32%	15%	101%	-50%
Angola	34%	15%	99%	-50%
Vietnam	27%	15%	98%	-49%
Nigeria	21%	14%	91%	-48%
Egypt, Arab Rep.	14%	14%	90%	-47%

Countries with low rates of money supply growth have low inflation rates.

Lowest Inflation countries in the world	Average Annual Money Supply growth	Average Annual Inflation (price increase)	Price increases over the 5 year period	Erosion in the Value of money over the period
Sweden	2.3%	1.6%	8%	-7%
France	4.9%	1.9%	10%	-9%
Chile	9.3%	1.9%	10%	-9%
Germany	0.1%	1.9%	10%	-9%
Morocco	8.3%	2.0%	10%	-9%
Portugal	8.3%	2.0%	10%	-9%
Canada	2.8%	2.0%	10%	-9%
United States	5.2%	2.4%	12%	-11%
Netherlands	4.2%	2.5%	13%	-11%
Norway	0.0%	2.5%	13%	-12%
Italy	7.6%	2.5%	13%	-12%
Finland	6.9%	2.6%	14%	-12%
Denmark	2.3%	2.6%	14%	-12%
Austria	1.4%	2.7%	14%	-12%
Bahamas	2.4%	2.7%	14%	-12%
Belgium	4.7%	2.8%	15%	-13%

Source: World Bank, IMF, Author.

Common tools employed by central banks to manage money supply (and inflation) include: (1) changing the interest rate at which it lends to banks, (2) buying and selling of government securities, and (3) setting reserve requirement ratios for banks.

Because the central bank has the power to create money, it also serves as the lender of last resort for banks (i.e., a lender that always has an ability to lend). The process of managing price levels is dynamic, and central banks have regular meetings to decide the most appropriate action to take in order to achieve their primary objective of maintaining price stability (and, subject to that, stimulating economic growth where possible). The methods of controlling money supply may be simple but delivering price stability year after year and through changing economic environments can be challenging. Maintaining effective control over price stability requires a strong and independent mandate from the government. An explicit political commitment and strong public interest in price stability can be instrumental in empowering a central bank to deliver on this challenging task. A good track record on price stability helps to anchor expectations of low price increases among the general public. An environment of low inflation expectations enhances the effectiveness of a central bank's policy actions aimed at delivering price stability in the future.

Changing interest rates on loans to financial institutions. In order to support the smooth running of banks, the central bank provides short-term loan facilities that banks can access at a particular interest rate. When the central bank fears that there is a risk of prices rising too fast (risk of high inflation) in a strong economic environment, it increases the interest rate at which it lends to banks and other financial institutions. Banks will then pass on the higher cost of credit to their customers, in the form of higher interest rates on consumer and business loans, and higher interest rates on customer deposits. Higher interest rates make it more attractive for people to save and more costly to borrow. When high interest rates encourage people and businesses to put money away (i.e., reduce the amount of readily accessible money in the economy), it reduces the rate of price increases (the inflation rate tends to fall). When the central bank is interested in stimulating the economy to raise price levels, it lowers the interest rate at which it lends to banks. Banks find it cheaper to borrow at this lower rate; consequently, they lower interest rates on their loans and deposits to reflect the lower cost of funds in the economy. Customers react to a lower cost of funds by saving less and borrowing more. These actions increase the amount of money in circulation and put upward pressure on the rate of price increases (a rising inflation rate).

Buying and selling of government bonds. When the central bank wants to increase the amount of money in circulation, it can print money and use the proceeds to buy government bonds. The sellers of the bonds receive money from the central bank and can readily use this money for their spending and investment needs. Central bank bond purchases increase the amount of money in circulation. When the central bank wants to reduce money supply, it can sell government bonds it has in stock, to soak up money from buyers. When individual and businesses use up a portion of their readily accessible cash or savings to buy these bonds, they will have less money to finance immediate spending and investment plans. By reducing the amount of money in circulation, central bank bond sales help to lower the rate of price increases in the economy.

Setting of reserve-requirement ratios for banks. One of the important roles of central banks is to regulate banks to ensure financial stability in the economy; a mechanism for doing so is to set reserve-requirement ratios for banks. Reserve requirements are minimum proportions of deposits that banks must keep in cash (i.e., not lend out) in order to maintain the ability to meet the cash withdrawal demands of depositors. When the central bank increases the reserve requirement ratio, banks will be required to keep a higher proportion of deposits in cash and therefore have less money to lend. A higher reserve requirement ratio depletes available lending resources and increases the cost of funds. Banks raise interest rates on deposits and loans to reflect the higher cost of funds. In response to high interest rates, consumers and businesses save more and borrow less. The lower amount of money in circulation (from changes in spending and borrowing habits) helps to lower the rate of price increases.

EXTREME EROSION IN THE VALUE OF MONEY. EXAMPLES FROM HISTORY: Germany, Brazil, Zimbabwe, and Venezuela

Germany (1921–1924). Instead of raising taxes to pay for costs associated with World War I, the German government decided to finance the payment of reparations primarily by borrowing. When this strategy became more challenging, the government provided itself with the flexibility to create money by abandoning the convertibility of its currency (the German mark) into gold. Removing the gold backing gave the government unlimited ability to create money. The ability to create money was so excessively abused that the currency lost its entire value over time and became completely worthless as a medium of exchange. From 1921, when the German government resorted to printing money to pay for war reparations, the massive increase in the supply of money resulted in a rapid and steep loss of value. Prices of basic goods more than tripled every month, and by the end of 1923, prices had risen by over 1 billion percent, a ridiculous amount (for all practical purposes). The price of a loaf of bread increased from about 1 mark in 1918 to 4 marks by 1921. The price of bread rose further to 160 marks by the end of 1922 and to 200 billion marks by the end of 1923. Prices of eggs, clothes, shoes, and other basic items followed a similar pattern.

Figure 8.4. German children playing with stacks of worthless money in the early 1920s.

Source: Wikipedia

For money to retain its value, it has to be limited in supply. In the early 1920s, the German government printed unlimited quantities of money, and the currency lost so much value that it had to be abandoned as a medium of exchange. By the end of 1923,

113

the German mark had lost its entire value. It simply became worthless. Before the war, one US dollar was worth about 4 marks. By the end of 1923, one needed over 4 trillion marks to buy one US dollar. Companies carried truckloads of money to pay workers several times a day. That way, workers' spouses could rush to the grocery store to quickly buy goods before they became unaffordable hours later. It was common to see people carrying money around in wheelbarrows or suitcases. The German people lost confidence in the currency and resorted to real assets and barter to facilitate exchange. The hyperinflation ended between late 1923 and early 1924; the old mark was suspended, and a new currency that was backed by real assets (gold in this case) was introduced to restore credibility. In converting to the new currency, twelve zeroes were erased from prices (i.e., one unit of the new currency was equivalent in value to 1 trillion units of the old currency).

Hyperinflation in Brazil (1980–1994). This period of high price increases began when the government resorted to printing money to finance its large spending plans. Initially the government could finance the deficit by borrowing money, but interest rates increased to prohibitive levels when lenders lost confidence in the sustainability of government spending habits. In 1990, economy-wide prices rose by 3000%. An item that cost 10 units of the currency at the beginning of year would cost 310 units by the end of the year. Effectively in that year alone, through government action, the currency lost most of its value. The loss of government credibility meant that the only currency the public could trust was one backed by real or external assets (e.g., the US dollar) that the government could not abuse. Between 1993 and 1994, the old currency was abandoned because it was no longer a viable medium of exchange. A new currency was introduced and widely adopted because it was initially pegged to the dollar, a currency Brazilians could trust because of the higher credibility of its issuer (the US central bank). The Brazilian government was essentially borrowing the credibility of the US central bank to restore a functioning medium of exchange in Brazil.

High inflation and hyperinflation in Zimbabwe (1999 to 2009). When Zimbabwe gained independence in 1980, the Zimbabwean dollar was worth more than the US dollar. From the late 1990s, the government of Zimbabwe pursued an indigenization policy to transfer ownership and control of farmlands and businesses from white owners to the indigenous black population. Over time, the uncertainty associated with this policy reduced investment, agricultural productivity, export revenue (tobacco exports accounted for a third of export revenue), and tax revenue. Falling productivity and weak economic growth reduce a government's sources of revenue, and the case of Zimbabwe was no exception. As the economy and government revenue contracted, instead of cutting its expenditure in line with falling revenue, the government became more dependent on printing money to finance its needs. Prices rose from 40 to 50 percent per year in the early part of the period, but they went out of control between 2008 and 2009, rising to levels in the millions of percent. Despite government efforts to print bills of higher denominations, the currency became so worthless that sackloads of bills were needed to buy basic items. In 2009, the Zimbabwean dollar was so worthless that it was officially abandoned as a medium of exchange. In place of a national currency, the

Zimbabwean government officially endorsed the US dollar and the South African rand to facilitate exchange. The government had lost so much credibility that citizens could no longer trust its ability to manage a national currency. The Zimbabwean example shows that the monopoly that a government enjoys over money supply is a privilege that can be lost when the government repeatedly abuses public trust.

Figure 8.5 The 100 trillion Zimbabwean dollar banknote.

This was the largest denomination ever produced and was issued in 2008 and 2009. It was worth about thirty U.S. dollars when it was issued, which reflects a total loss of value compared to the early 1980s, when one Zimbabwe dollar was worth more than one US dollar.

Source: Wikipedia

High inflation in Venezuela (beginning in 2012). Venezuela is one of the largest petroleum exporters in the world and has benefitted from the rise in oil prices over the prior decade. However, growing government intervention in the economy, in the form of subsidies, price controls, takeovers of private businesses, and large welfare spending have raised government spending well above government revenue. Excessive government intervention has depleted the productive capacity of the economy and made the country more dependent on imported goods to satisfy basic consumption needs. By 2012–2013, the government's budget deficit rose to unsustainable levels (over 10% of GDP). Shortages of basic goods such as toilet paper, sugar, flour, and cooking oil became common, and long queues in supermarkets became part of the daily routine for most Venezuelans. The government reacted to the shortage of basic items by deploying the army to take over factories, shops, and other businesses. The government officially devalued its currency, but the shortage of dollars in the economy prompted some to resort to buying dollars in the black market (the only true market that allowed "free" exchange of dollars was an illegal one). The black market valued the Venezuelan bolivar at much lower rates than the official government exchange rate, which restricted access to dollars. As prices increased and the purchasing power of consumers declined, Venezuela plunged into social and political unrest with a large number of demonstrations and political protests in 2014. The government's strict exchange-rate controls and its determination to set prices of basic goods in the economy pressured many firms to cut down production; some had to close their entire operations because they were no longer viable. According to official statistics, prices in Venezuela increased by 60 to 70% in 2014, and some suggest that the official numbers may grossly underestimate the true level of price increases—or the erosion in purchasing power—that Venezuelans have experienced.

9

INTEREST RATES AND EXCHANGE RATES

Interest rates determine the financial compensation that borrowers pay to lenders. In order to encourage people and firms to provide capital, they need to be adequately compensated for risks they assume by deferring immediate consumption and for risks associated with the investments that they fund. When the financial compensation associated with lending increases, saving money can become a more attractive use of excess income than immediate consumption. People respond to rising interest rates by saving more and spending less. On the other hand, when interest rates fall to low levels, saving and lending become less attractive.

FACTORS THAT DETERMINE THE APPROPRIATE LEVEL OF FINANCIAL COMPENSATION OR RATE OF INTEREST ON BORROWINGS

In the process of making a loan, a lender faces a number of risks. A lender will require adequate financial compensation to cover these risks before he provides capital. The risks assumed by lenders include:

1.   **Default Risk.** This is the largest source of risk for a lender. If the borrower is unable or unwilling to pay, the lender could lose the full amount of the loan. Lenders will therefore demand financial compensation that reflects the risk of default of the borrower. The financial return to a lender is capped by the interest rate he charges on loans. But in the event of a default, a lender may lose the entire capital in the loan. As a result, the risk appetite of lenders is limited. When the risk of default becomes too high, lending becomes unattractive even at high interest rates.

2.   **Inflation risk or the risk of erosion in purchasing power**. When a person lends money directly or provides capital that is used by financial intermediaries (e.g., banks) to lend, he is essentially giving away his current purchasing power (current consumption ability) in exchange for acquiring purchasing power in the future. Because the purchasing power of money is eroded whenever prices rise, a lender will demand adequate compensation to protect his purchasing power from the risk of inflation. Inflation expectations are instrumental in determining the level of interest rates in the economy. In situations where prices rise too fast, the risk of eroding one's purchasing power may

become too high, and lending becomes unattractive. The risk of losing one's purchasing power increases with the term of a loan. When the inflation risk is too high, lending activity slows down and may be restricted to short durations covering a few months to one or two years.

3. **The term or duration of a loan.** Borrowing involves a contract that specifies exactly when the loan should be repaid and the periodic rate of interest that needs to be paid on the loan. A lender may not have access to his or her capital until the loan is repaid in full. In some cases, a lender may not be able to exchange the loan for cash during the intermediate period. Where an exchange is possible, (e.g. in countries with developed financial markets), lenders may face uncertainty over the potential selling price. Lenders demand higher financial compensation on loans that mature over longer periods. Default risk as well as the risk of purchasing power erosion rise with the duration of a loan. As a result, interest rates are generally higher for long-term loans.

4. **Liquidity risk**. A financial instrument such as a loan is said to be liquid when it can be sold at any time for a fair price. The ability to convert a loan into cash can be useful, because a lender's financial profile may change and the lender may end up in a position of requiring capital. A change in a lender's assessment of the credit worthiness of a borrower may also alter the lender's willingness to hold onto a loan. Liquidity allows a lender the flexibility to change his or her mind on the decision to provide capital to a particular borrower. This flexibility comes with minor penalties, because lenders can sell their loans at a fair price in a liquid market. Lenders are more likely to demand higher financial compensation (interest rates) when they cannot readily sell loans for cash. Loans to the government and large corporations (government and corporate bonds) are standardized and easily tradable in financial markets. These loans have the highest liquidity. In an environment of stable prices, adequate levels of liquidity can increase the willingness of capital providers to lend over an extended period.

Government borrowings are protected from the risk of default. Loans made to the government carry the lowest risk of all loans because they are protected from the risk of default. Government borrowings are commonly referred to as "risk-free" loans (or "risk-free" securities) and interest rates associated with government borrowings are often referred to as "risk-free" rates. Loans made to the government are considered to be free from the risk of default, because the government, theoretically, has unlimited ability to create money and raise taxes to repay loans issued in its own currency. Of all possible borrowers, a government is the only borrower who has the ability to pay interest and repay the loan in full with absolute certainty. Supported by its protection from the risk of default, the market for issuing and trading government bonds is often the first to develop and the largest financial product market in many economies. When a government borrows in a foreign currency, the loans are no longer protected from the risk of default. This is because while a government has control over printing money in its own currency, it has no control over money supply in foreign currencies.

The level of interest rates in an economy is primarily determined by inflation expectations. Loans made to the government may be free from the risk of default, but they carry other risks. For example, a person may be guaranteed to get his money back from the government, but the financial compensation on these loans may not be enough to fully compensate for the loss of purchasing power experienced during the term of the loan. When the risk of default is not in question, the lowest interest rate or financial compensation that a lender can possibly demand is one that compensates for the loss of his purchasing power (i.e., from price increases) during the term of the loan.

Capital providers will require an interest rate that, at the very least, compensates for the expected erosion in the value of money over the term of the loan. Therefore even for the lowest risk borrowings in the economy (i.e., government bonds that are free from the risk of default), the lowest sustainable interest rate has to, at least compensate for the risk of inflation. In other words, the real interest rate or inflation adjusted interest rate has to structurally be greater than (or equal to) 0%. Real rates that are less than 0% (i.e., interest rates that are lower than expected inflation rates) are not sustainable because capital providers who end up losing their purchasing power may withdraw from lending, and the shortage of funds will push up interest rates. Government policies that lead to high inflation and rising inflation expectations raise the level of interest rates on all lending in the economy (including loans made to the government). In countries where lenders have less confidence in a government's ability to maintain price stability, they often demand high real rates (higher levels of interest rates when compared to inflation rates) in order to compensate for greater uncertainty in preserving the purchasing power of capital.

Interest rates on government bonds set the benchmark for all lending in the economy. Because they are free from the risk of default, loans made to the government are the lowest risk loans in an economy, and they carry the lowest interest rates. As a result, interest rates associated with government borrowings (risk-free rates) are used as benchmarks or reference interest rates for all loans in the economy. For example, when the government pursues inflationary policies, this translates into higher borrowing costs not just for the government but for all private citizens and businesses and reduces investment activity below its potential.

Lending to individuals and businesses carries higher risks than lending to the government. Unlike the government, private citizens do not have the ability to print money or raise taxes, and they may be unable to repay loans in times of difficulty. Because of their higher risk of default, capital providers require higher compensation (interest rates) for lending to private entities. The degree to which the borrowing rate of individuals and firms differs from the risk-free benchmark depends on their ability to service and repay loans. Credit worthiness can be assessed by examining the prospects of household income or business profits. Firms that experience high levels of profitability and workers who command strong wage levels in industries that are relatively stable, are more likely to access loans at attractive interest rates. Since the rate of interest (the return to the lender or the cost to the borrower) ought to compensate for the riskiness of the loan, interest rates tend to rise as the credit quality of the borrower deteriorates and the term of the loan increases. The financial return for lending is capped by the interest rates charged on loans but in the event of a default, lenders may lose all the capital tied to a loan. Because of the risk of large potential losses, lenders are primarily interested in providing capital to high quality or credit worthy borrowers. The least credit worthy borrowers may struggle to access loans even when then they are prepared to pay high interest rates.

Excessive government borrowing can raise the level of interest rates in an economy. In most countries, governments borrow to finance part of their spending needs. When the government's appetite for borrowing rises too fast, it may consume an increasing share of the available savings in the economy. When excessive government borrowing depletes savings resources in a country, households and businesses will only provide additional funds (sourced from further cuts to current consumption) when they are compensated with high levels of interest rates. By driving up interest rates and utilizing most of the savings resources in an economy, excessive government spending and borrowing restricts access to capital for private individuals and businesses.

EXCHANGE RATES

International trade has the potential to improve the well-being of citizens in all countries. In the same way that a national currency facilitates trade within a country, currencies such as the US dollar and the euro are widely employed to facilitate international trade. Unlike national currencies, most governments have no control over the supply of currencies employed in international trade. Firms that are interested in purchasing goods and services produced in other countries need to exchange their national currency for international currencies. A country earns foreign exchange (i.e. international currencies) when it exports goods and services to other countries. Foreign exchange can also be earned by attracting investment from foreign countries.

The degree to which governments, citizens, and businesses in a country can consume goods produced in other countries depends on the level of their foreign-currency earnings. When a country's foreign-exchange earnings far exceed its foreign-exchange spending needs, the excess supply of foreign exchange may support an appreciation of the domestic currency (relative to international currencies) and encourage greater demand for foreign products. When money appreciates in value, fewer units are required to purchase an item. When the domestic currency appreciates relative to foreign currencies, demand for imported goods may rise because imported goods become cheaper (i.e., fewer units of domestic currency are required to purchase the same imported product).

When a country's foreign-exchange requirements fall short of its foreign-exchange earnings, the foreign-exchange deficit (or excess demand for international currencies), may put pressure on the domestic currency to depreciate (relative to foreign currencies). A currency depreciates or loses value when more units are needed to purchase an item. An insufficient supply of foreign exchange, forces the value of foreign currencies to rise (relative to the domestic currency). A higher price of foreign exchange translates into a higher price for imported goods and services. When prices of imported goods rise sharply, demand tends to fall in an effort to restore the foreign-currency balance in the economy to more sustainable levels.

Foreign exchange requirements are driven by consumption and investment needs that are satisfied by purchasing goods from international markets. When international prices of key imported products rise sharply, foreign currency earnings may no longer be sufficient to meet higher spending requirements. This may cause the domestic currency to depreciate in value in order to restore a healthier balance between foreign currency earnings and spending. When international prices of key imported products fall, this can reduce foreign exchange spending requirements and support a stable (or stronger) exchange rate.

The quantity of exports as well as international prices of a country's exports affect the value of foreign currency earnings. When the international price of a country's exports rise sharply, this can meaningfully increase foreign exchange earnings and cause the domestic currency to appreciate in value (relative to international currencies). On the other hand, falling international prices for a country's exports will depress foreign currency earnings. When falling foreign currency earnings are no longer adequate to meet spending requirements, the domestic currency may fall in value relative to international currencies in order to restore a healthier balance.

The exchange rate between a domestic currency and an international currency tends to move in a direction that aims at balancing a country's foreign-exchange spending requirements with its foreign-exchange earnings. When foreign-exchange spending requirements far exceed foreign-exchange earnings, the domestic currency tends to depreciate to make foreign products more costly. When foreign-exchange earnings are considerably larger than spending requirements, the domestic currency tends to appreciate to make foreign products more attractive in price.

The illusionary wealth impact of inflationary policies may drive foreign currency deficits to unsustainable levels. When the government prints too much money, prices of goods and services in the economy rise to reflect the erosion in the value of money. More units of the national currency are required to buy the same item, because money has lost value. Unless there is a corresponding depreciation of the domestic currency relative to foreign currencies to reflect the erosion in the value of money, foreign goods may become cheaper in the short-term. When the erosion in the value of money is not fully reflected in the exchange rate, the relative cheapness of imported products can produce a temporary wealth-effect, because imported items in a typical consumption basket may become cheaper in real terms. Consumers may also take further advantage by shifting their consumption patterns towards foreign products. Unless there is a proportionate depreciation in the exchange rate to reflect the erosion in the value of money, prices of imported products, in a typical consumer basket, may rise more slowly when compared to price increases of locally produced goods. As a result, official inflation figures may understate the extent to which the value of money has been eroded.

When wage and price increases are not supported by gains in productivity, the illusion of wealth that arises when the government prints too much money wears off over time. When the exchange rate does not adjust to fully reflect the erosion in the value of the domestic currency, prices of goods produced in a country rise faster than imported products. Higher price increases for domestically produced goods make them more expensive for both local residents and foreign buyers. In response to higher prices, foreign buyers may reduce their demand for a country's exports. Declining export activity reduces the foreign-currency earnings of a country. At the same time, rising appetite for imported products increases foreign-currency spending requirements. If this trend continues, foreign-currency earnings may no longer be sufficient to cover foreign currency spending requirements and the domestic currency may need to adjust to restore a healthier balance.

Governments can take foreign loans to satisfy foreign-exchange spending needs in the short-term, but borrowing is not a sustainable method of funding large foreign-exchange deficits. A shortage of foreign currency in an economy pressures the local currency to depreciate in an effort to restore a balance between foreign-currency earnings and spending requirements. When the foreign-currency deficit is large, the domestic currency can sometimes undergo a drastic erosion in value in its exchange rate, to reflect the long-term compounded impact of a government's inflationary policies.

A sharp depreciation of a local currency magnifies the loss of purchasing power that is associated with periods of high inflation. By the time exchange rates adjust to reflect the full effect of the erosion in the value of money, household consumption baskets may have been heavily tilted toward foreign products. As a result, a sharp depreciation of the domestic currency has the potential to erode the purchasing power of households to a large degree. Overall, consumption may fall sharply due to the loss of purchasing power, and consumers may be pressured to migrate towards locally produced goods. The weakness of the currency also makes locally produced goods cheaper for foreign buyers and promotes demand for a country's exports. Growing exports and declining appetite for imported products can restore a healthy balance between a country's foreign-currency earnings and its foreign-currency expenditure.

Exchange-rate adjustments play a crucial role in restoring the fundamental level of purchasing power within an economy. Exchange-rate adjustments help to correct for the illusion of purchasing power gains that can arise from high inflation policies. Rather than focusing on implementing prudent economic policies, governments are sometimes tempted to restore economic confidence by excessively intervening in currency markets or arbitrarily fixing their exchange rates. When exchange rates are not allowed to adjust freely to reflect economic fundamentals, the effects of illusions created by inflation policies and other unsustainable economic policies can compound over a long period and ultimately result in a dramatic economic meltdown when the inevitable adjustment occurs.

Adjustments in currency markets to reflect the erosion in the value of money that arises from inflation policies is absolutely necessary to reset the fundamental purchasing power within an economy. If exchange rates could be held back from adjusting to reflect the erosion in the value of money, governments that pursue high inflation policies will be delivering the strongest gains in international purchasing power to their citizens. This illusion cannot hold over any extended period.

Sustainable gains in purchasing power can only be derived from productivity gains.

The level of international trade between countries continues to grow. The typical household consumption basket as well as inputs and services for businesses are becoming more global in nature. Due to rising international trade, the effects of a large and swift currency adjustment can be felt by a broader segment of the domestic economy and can sometimes create high levels of economic uncertainty. Businesses that are directly involved in exporting and importing products and countries that are major exporters or importers in the global economy are likely to face the greatest shocks from sharp currency adjustments. Currencies can adjust for a number of reasons. However it is important to emphasize that the most dramatic adjustments are often a direct result of poor economic policies and are more likely to occur in countries that have a history of high inflation rates.

Exchange rate adjustment may be necessary to restore levels of fundamental purchasing power in an economy. To further illustrate the importance of exchange-rate adjustments, imagine an economy that grows at a steady *real* rate of 5% every year and where the average income per capita or income for the average worker is $1,000. At the beginning of the period, assume one unit of the country's currency was exchangeable for one dollar. The government decided to pursue a high inflation policy in an effort to support its spending plans and to boost economic growth. Without the support of proportionate productivity gains, increases in money supply ultimately lead to high inflation. Money-supply growth failed to lift the rate of productivity gains in the economy.

The economy continued to grow at 5% in real terms, and inflation rates rose to 15% a year for the following decade. When the price of domestically produced goods rises by 15% every year, this means that the domestic currency is losing about 13% of its value every year within the economy. One requires 1.15 times more units of currency to purchase the same item after a year. The average worker received annual wage increases of 20%. This consisted of a 5% increase derived from productivity gains (a real increase) and a 15% increase driven primarily by money-supply growth and inflation (i.e., the 15% increase was not underpinned by real value creation in the economy). Also assume that the inflation rate in the United States economy is 0% (perfect price stability) and that, all imported products have stable international prices.

In a scenario where the exchange rate does not adjust, while the domestic currency is losing value when compared to goods produced locally, the currency still maintains its purchasing power in international markets. As a result of compounding 20% wage increases over ten years, the average worker's income would increase to over $6,000 even though his productivity gains (5% per year) can only justify an income of $1,600 in ten years. Because wages are rising much faster than international prices, workers and households in this country would substantially increase their international purchasing power over ten years (from $1,000 to $6,000). Due to the 15% annual price increase in the domestic economy, in the absence of currency adjustment, domestic goods that initially cost one dollar to produce, will more than quadruple in cost to over four dollars within a decade. When currencies do not adjust to correct for domestic inflation policies, the considerable increase in the price of domestically produced goods makes them less affordable to international buyers, and the volume of exports is likely to decline substantially. On the other hand, because international goods are more stable in price, the substantial increase in wages (in the absence of currency adjustment) increases the international purchasing power of household by a considerable proportion and makes the importation of goods more attractive than domestic production.

If this situation continued into the future, *it would mean that the international purchasing power of the country's residents can continue to rise at double digit rates forever.* In practice such an illusion cannot be sustained. It is more likely that the currency would adjust such that the purchasing power of workers would move closer to levels that can be justified based on productivity gains (or real growth rates). The domestic currency may need to depreciate by a considerable amount, to correct for the illusionary effect of inflation on income levels over the 10 year period. A depreciation of about 70% is required to reset the purchasing power to levels that can be justified by productivity improvements (i.e., to reflect a purchasing power of $1,600 rather than $6,000). When currencies are allowed to adjust freely, this depreciation can occur smoothly over time, and the economy is likely to be more stable. When the government intervenes excessively in currency markets, it may only be able to hold back the adjustment temporarily. This is because there are substantial costs associated with intervention in currency markets. Intervention ultimately results in larger and sharper adjustments that increase economic instability.

Countries that pursue high inflation policies have currencies that depreciate most of the time to correct for the illusionary effect of high price increases. In such countries, there is certainty over currency depreciation over an extended period, even though the rate of adjustment may be less certain.

Interest Rate Parity. In a globalized world with free movement of capital, in the absence of exchange rate adjustments, it would be possible to make large profits by borrowing money from countries with low interest rates to invest in countries with high interest rates. Following on from the previous example, let us assume one year interest rates of 16% in the high inflation country (i.e., a 1% real rate in an environment of 15% annual inflation) and 1% in the United States (i.e., 1% real rate in an environment of 0% inflation). If there is no risk of currency devaluation, anyone can borrow money at 1% in the U.S., exchange the dollar proceeds for the equivalent amount in local currency of the high inflation country, deposit the money in a bank at 16% interest rate, and at the end of the year, repatriate the proceeds back to the U.S. and pocket a 15% return without taking any risk.

Interest rate parity is a theory that suggests that the opportunity to make attractive returns with no exchange rate risk cannot persist and in order for this profit opportunity to be eliminated, the currency of the high inflation country would have depreciate by 15% in one year. In other words, exchange rates need to adjust to reflect the difference in interest rates (or inflation rates) between two countries. There are several other factors that influence the value of exchange rates in the short-term so that, the exchange rate adjustment required to maintain interest rate parity may not occur over short periods. However over extended periods, exchange rates adjust in the direction predicted by interest rate parity. Currencies of countries with high inflation and high interest rates depreciate over time (relative to currencies of countries that maintain stable prices or low inflation).

For countries that are primarily dependent on commodity exports for foreign exchange earnings, changes in commodity prices can have a meaningful impact on exchange rates and international purchasing power. Commodities are global products and are priced in international currencies. When commodities are a key part of a country's economic output and exports, rising commodity prices increase the value of economic output and foreign currency earnings. Rising foreign currency earnings increase the international purchasing power of the country's residents. A considerable increase in foreign currency earnings may support the local currency to appreciate (or stabilize in value) relative to international currencies. An environment of high commodity prices and strong economic growth can also help such countries attract significant foreign investment (to exploit natural resources or take advantage of other opportunities in the economy), which can further boost foreign exchange resources in the economy.

On the other hand, when commodity prices fall sharply, this can reduce foreign currency earnings by a considerable amount and create a large imbalance between foreign currency spending requirements and foreign currency earnings. A drastic reduction in foreign currency earnings may put pressure on domestic currencies to depreciate. A weaker exchange rates reduces the purchasing power of local residents for international goods. In this case, exchange rates also adjust to link the international purchasing power of a country to the value of its exports. A country's foreign currency earnings has a significant influence over its international purchasing power, therefore when falling commodity prices reduce foreign exchange earnings, the exchange rate tends to adjust to reflect the lower level of international purchasing power of the country's residents.

Currencies adjust to reflect changes in the international purchasing power of a country. For major commodity exporters, rising commodity prices increase foreign exchange earnings and a country's international purchasing power. For major commodity exporters, domestic currencies will tend to appreciate (relative to international currencies) during periods of rising commodity prices and depreciate during periods of falling commodity prices.

When major commodity exporters also pursue high inflation policies, the positive impact of rising commodity prices may somewhat offset the negative impact of high inflation on the value of domestic currencies. A high inflation rate puts pressure on currencies to depreciate to reflect the erosion in the value of money relative to currencies in countries that maintain price stability. With the offsetting support of strong foreign currency earnings, during periods of high commodity prices, local currencies may depreciate at slower rates or may remain stable in value. This may be in contrast to low inflation commodity exporters that are more likely to experience currency appreciation in an environment of rising commodity prices. When a major commodity exporter pursues high inflation policies, local currencies can depreciate sharply during periods of falling commodity prices. When foreign exchange earnings fall sharply as a result of declining commodity prices, both the inflation adjustment and the commodity adjustment are in the same direction and can result in an accelerated depreciation of local currencies to reflect a major drop in international purchasing power.

There is considerable scope for governments to employ prudent economic policies to smoothen the impact of the commodity cycle. A government that saves a meaningful portion of robust revenues and foreign exchange earnings during periods of rising commodity prices, would have greater potential to maintain the international purchasing power of residents when commodity prices fall. Countries that build strong international currency reserves and save money (e.g. to reduce debt) during periods of high commodity prices, have greater ability to support more stable exchange rates when commodity prices fall.

Large currency fluctuations may more often be a delayed sign of policy failure than market overreaction. Extreme currency movements are more common in countries that pursue unsustainable economic policies. When a government pursues high inflation policies, prices of locally produced goods rise rapidly to reflect the erosion in the value of money. One would expect that the erosion in the value of the domestic currency should be equally reflected in the exchange rate. If the value of a currency has been eroded, just as more units of the currency is required to buy goods (i.e., prices rise), so should more units of the currency be required to buy a unit of any stable foreign currency. In other words, stable exchange rates are more likely to be realized in countries that have a good track record of maintaining price stability (i.e., those that support an environment of low and stable inflation rates). When major commodity exporters are too eager to spend robust revenues and foreign exchange earnings during periods of high commodity prices, they may be setting themselves up for sharp depreciation in exchange rates and a major drop in international purchasing power when commodity prices fall.

In practice, exchange rates between currencies may not readily adjust. Exchange rates may be slow in adjusting to the erosion in the value of money, because governments can attract large amounts of foreign investment or borrow in international markets to fulfill excess foreign-currency spending requirements. So long as foreign investors are willing to plug the deficit, the exchange rate (i.e., the number of units of domestic currency that is required to purchase a unit of foreign currency) may not fully adjust to reflect the extent to which the value of money has been eroded in the local economy. However, running large foreign exchange deficits makes a currency more vulnerable to swift and large adjustments. The exchange rate can adjust rapidly when foreign investors lose confidence in the management of the economy and the government is no longer able to borrow in international markets to cover the foreign exchange deficit. When access to foreign capital is restricted, currencies become prone to a sharp adjustment to reflect the effects of inflationary policies that may have lasted several years. For major commodity exporters, the ability to attract international capital if often linked to the commodity price environment. Greater access to international capital during periods of rising commodity prices may support a government's efforts to plug the foreign exchange deficit that arises from excessive demand for imported goods. For such countries, access to international capital is often restricted in an environment of low commodity prices. Because the exchange rate of the domestic currency may have been unsustainably supported at a high level, the combined effect of lower commodity prices and restricted access to international capital may lead to a sharp depreciation.

The sharp unraveling in currency markets catches more attention than the gradual erosion in the value of money that people experience through regular price increases. Governments and politicians tend to ignore local price increases but become overly alarmed when currency markets finally catch up and exchange rates equally reflect the erosion in the value of money. However, the compounded effect of continued price increases in eroding the purchasing power of citizens could be equally alarming.

Swift adjustments in exchange rates attract more attention when they occur. However, when analyzed over an extended period, the degree of exchange rate adjustments may be comparable to the erosion in the value of money in the domestic economy.

Figure 9.1 shows that money-supply growth is highly influential in determining the level of inflation and interests rates and the degree of exchange rate adjustments (relative to currencies of countries with stable prices) in a country.

Figure 9.1. Money supply growth determines the rate of inflation, the level of interest rates and exchange rate volatility in an economy

Countries ranked by money supply growth (lowest to highest)	Money Supply Growth 2010-2013	Consumer Price Increases 2010-2013	Annual Interest Rate on 10 year Government Bonds (2014)	Rate of Currency Appreciation or Depreciation Relative to the US Dollar 2010-2014
Germany	-3%	7%	1%	-10%
United Kingdom	2%	14%	2%	0%
United States	13%	9%	2%	-
Korea	23%	11%	3%	9%
South Africa	29%	22%	8%	-33%
Nigeria	46%	53%	13%	-20%
Mexico	48%	16%	6%	-15%
Brazil	73%	25%	12%	-28%
Indonesia	74%	23%	8%	-23%
India	74%	48%	9%	-40%
Turkey	83%	35%	10%	-34%
Russia	95%	30%	10%	-25%
Ghana*	164%	47%	25%	-56%
Argentina*	187%	50%	22%	-55%
Venezuela*	349%	175%	18%	-66%

*10 year bond data not available. Filled with interest rates on government borrowing of less than 10 years

Source: IMF, central banks, author

Comparing the attractions of interest rates and investment returns across countries can be challenging. Every government has a strong influence over the rate of price increases (the inflation rate) and the level of interest rates that prevail in an economy. When comparing the attractiveness of investment returns in a country, one has to take account of the rate of inflation and the level of interest rates associated with government borrowings in that country. At the very least, capital providers will expect to be compensated for the potential loss of purchasing power from price increases. Interest rates in an economy will therefore be closely linked to expected inflation rates. If a government is running a high inflationary policy, this can create an illusion of gain that exaggerates the attractiveness of returns on most investments.

When the rate of inflation is high in a country, money loses value at a fast pace. To reflect the erosion in the value of money, prices of all assets rise sharply over time. Price increases primarily reflect the erosion in the value of money and may not be representative of changes in the fundamental value of assets. In such a country, the nominal return or profitability on most investments is likely to be high when measured in units of that currency. Comparing nominal rates of return across countries can be misleading especially when there is a wide divergence in monetary policy, inflation rates, and interest rates.

For example, a 10% return on an investment in a country with a stable 2% inflation rate and a 3% government-bond rate could be far more attractive (i.e., an 8% real rate/increase in purchasing power and a 7% return above the risk-free rate) than a similar investment (in the same industry) in a higher inflation country that generates a return of 20% when the inflation rate in that country is 15% and the government-bond rate is 17%. In the higher inflation country, the real (i.e., inflation-adjusted) return on the investment is only 5%. In order to create economic value, firms need to grow revenues and profits in real or inflation-adjusted terms. In the low inflation country (i.e., inflation rate of 2%), a firm that generates 5% revenue and profit growth would have created economic value in real terms whereas a firm in the high inflation country that generates a much stronger revenue and profit growth of 10% would have eroded economic value in real terms. To generate a comparable level of real economic value, the firm in the high inflation country would need to grow its revenues by 18% (i.e., a real revenue growth rate of 3% + an inflation rate of 15%)

When the value of money is not stable, an increase in prices or profits may not represent an increase in value.

Governments that pursue unsustainable economic policies create greater uncertainty in exchange rates. Exchange-rate risks further compound the difficulties of comparing the attractiveness of investment opportunities across different countries.

Integrity in managing the value of money and the economy pays attractive long-term dividends

In countries that have embraced a commitment to price stability and integrity in the management of economic affairs, high levels of public trust in price stability encourage people to save and support a sustainable environment of low and stable interest rates. The ability of a government to borrow at low interest rates for long periods of time (i.e., the ability to take 10 to 30 year loans) to finance long-term investments provides major benefits to an economy. Low and stable interest rates can stimulate economic and employment growth by helping governments, businesses, and households to access low-cost funding for investment activity. Borrowing for such long periods is only possible because of the high levels of public confidence in the credibility of prudent government policies. The populace will also supply these funds when they have great confidence in the ability of the government to deliver price stability on a sustainable basis. Because citizens and firms lock in their savings at low fixed-interest rates, any risk of high inflation could wipe out the real purchasing power of their savings. An environment of low and stable interest rates can only be built on a solid foundation of public trust—trust that is earned over a long period of time and is only visible in countries that have managed to deliver a long track record in monetary integrity and price stability. The high level of public trust also reveals itself in interest-rate levels that are closer to the levels of inflation in the economy i.e., low real or inflation-adjusted interest rates.

Countries with a poor monetary-policy framework and track record on price stability tend to have high and unstable interest rates, and their governments (the lowest-risk borrowers) struggle to borrow for long periods. The populace may only be willing to extend loans to the government for a few years, and, even when this is possible, the majority of lending to the government is concentrated in very short-term maturities and at high interest rates. In such countries, it more common for interest rates on government bonds to far exceed inflation rates (i.e., high real or inflation-adjusted interest rates). Lack of appetite in lending for long periods and a demand for a high level of financial compensation for risk-free government borrowings reflect low levels of public trust in a country's policy framework and the uncertainty that people face in protecting the real value of their capital, a risk that compounds as the term of a loan increases.

A government's ability to take long-term loans at low and stable interest rates is highly beneficial to households and businesses. Because interest rates associated with government borrowing set the benchmark for all lending activity in an economy, low-interest rates on long-term government borrowings facilitate access to long-term funds at attractive rates for households and businesses. When government-bond rates are too high or not available for long durations, lenders struggle to come up with lending rates for private businesses. Banks and other lenders need a reference interest rate in order to price loans. The interest rate associated with loans of any particular duration to an individual or business will typically consist of the government-bond rate (at that duration) plus some extra return to compensate for higher risks (such as the risk of default) associated with lending to private citizens and businesses.

When the government is unable to borrow for long periods, it closes the opportunity for private citizens to access funding for long-term investments. In countries with low and stable interest rates, most home buyers take long-term mortgage loans to buy houses. Low interest rates make it possible for households to enjoy the comfort of a home by providing a relatively small, upfront cash deposit and spreading the rest of the cost over fifteen to thirty years. Spreading payment over such long periods makes home ownership affordable and more accessible for the majority of households. In countries with high and volatile interest rates, loans to buy houses are either not available or are only available at high interest rates for very short terms (two to five years) and are therefore not appealing for most households. Households may need to save up for decades before they can enjoy the comfort of their own home. The "high cost" of acquiring a house may reduce investment in housing relative to its potential. Access to long-term funds at low interest rates increases the ability of firms to capitalize on investment opportunities. If businesses had to depend solely on their profits to fund investment opportunities, this would significantly reduce the level of investment activity in the economy. The process of saving internal cash flows to fund investments may take a long time and some large investments may no longer be feasible.

The long-term dividends associated with prudent monetary and fiscal policy far outweigh any illusionary short-term gains and the inevitable economic disruption associated with inflationary policies. The level of investment in countries that pursue high inflation policies is likely to be substantially lower than comparable countries that maintain price stability and support an environment of low interest rates. Because of the long track record required to create public trust in price stability and deliver a sustainable environment of low and stable inflation and interest rates, erratic policy changes and short-term attempts at reverting to prudent policies are unlikely to deliver the full extent of potential benefits.

When a government loses the confidence of investors because of poor economic policies, its access to funding may become restricted. In extreme cases, a government may only be able to access funding by borrowing against the credibility of foreign governments or institutions that have earned the trust of public investors. Credible governments or institutions that have earned high levels of public trust inspire investor confidence by pledging to monitor economic policies of governments that are no longer able to access funds on their own. Sponsoring governments and institutions demand a far greater standard of policy integrity and accountability than citizens of the finance-constrained governments demand on a regular basis.

For example, following the recent global financial crisis (2007–2010), the cost of borrowing for many southern European countries increased because of concerns about weak government finances and their dependence on large amounts of borrowing to finance government spending plans. Eventually, the public commitment of the European Central bank (a credible institution) to take a more active role in demanding greater financial discipline in the spending habits of these governments was instrumental in raising investor confidence and lowering the cost of borrowing for these countries.

Many developing countries turn to institutions such as the International Monetary Fund

(IMF) when their own credibility becomes too poor to attract funding from domestic and international capital providers. As a precondition for lending, the IMF typically imposes more prudent government spending plans (in line with government revenue), demands greater monetary integrity, and actively monitors and reports on a government's commitment to the new policy measures. When a government signs up to an IMF program and agrees to the higher level of policy integrity, in addition to direct loans provided by the IMF, the monitoring role of the institution provides an important endorsement that improves investor confidence and opens access to greater financial resources from domestic and international capital providers.

Integrity is the bedrock of sustainable economic policies, and citizens should take a greater role in demanding high levels of policy integrity. The process of outsourcing policy integrity to credible foreign governments and institutions typically creates short-term and potentially unsustainable solutions. The involvement of institutions such as the IMF in an economy is only initiated after long periods of economic mismanagement. Partly due to the large legacy costs associated with poor government policies, the introduction of prudent economic policies under such institutions may sometimes have an adverse short-term impact on living standards. Without the support of the general public, externally driven policy measures may not be sustainable. By outsourcing responsibility for correcting the effects of poor economic policies, instead of sowing the seeds of long-term policy integrity, the IMF, in some cases becomes a sacrificial lamb used by politicians to absorb the public discontent that arises as a direct result of the effects of poor economic policies.

In countries that have a poor history on economic governance, some governments may be tempted to give up their monopoly over money supply (i.e., the ability to use a national currency) in exchange for the right to use currencies of countries that have delivered a long track record of price stability. For example, a number of countries in Latin America (e.g. Argentina, Brazil, Ecuador, and Peru) have, at some point in their history, pegged their national currencies to the U.S. dollar and in some cases, allowed for extensive use of dollars as a primary currency, in an effort to deliver stable prices after going through long periods of extraordinary price increases (hyperinflation). Many southern European countries were eager to abandon their national currencies to embrace the Euro. The Euro presented them with the opportunity to borrow on the credibility of the European Central Bank, to access loans at low interest rates.

However in many of these examples, lessons from history show that borrowing on the credibility of foreign institutions is no panacea for the inability of citizens and their governments to deliver on policy integrity. For example, when Argentina decided to peg its currency to the U.S. dollar in 1991, following long periods of hyperinflation, this delivered price stability and a material improvement in living standards for some time. However, because of excessive government borrowing to finance large spending programs, Argentina could no longer afford to maintain the dollar peg. The eventual unwind of the peg, plunged Argentina into one of the deepest economic crisis in its history. In 2001, the Argentine peso was heavily devalued and Argentina was forced to default on its foreign debt obligations (because it could no longer afford to repay the loans). In some cases, the opportunity for southern European countries to borrow on the credibility of the European Central Bank would eventually be abused to finance unsustainable government spending programs. Eventually, excessive borrowing plunged a number of these countries into a prolonged economic crisis that depressed living standards. These examples illustrate the fact that, outsourcing policy integrity is not a strong foundation for economic stability. Citizens ultimately bear the cost for poor economic decisions and should therefore take greater interest in monitoring to ensure greater integrity in the way the government manages public finances and the economy.

10

SAVING AND INVESTMENT

Investment involves putting away resources from current consumption in order to derive a future benefit. The decision to invest in a particular venture is only taken when the potential future benefit exceeds the benefits associated with current consumption and other alternative uses of one's resources. For example, students (or their parents) decide to invest in higher education not just for the opportunity for intellectual development, but also to enhance the students' future employability and wage prospects. They believe that the investment will more than compensate for alternative opportunities, such as employment earnings that would have to be foregone in the interest of pursuing higher education. Many firms may have an opportunity to invest excess cash flows in bank deposits, in financial securities such as government bonds, or invest in their own businesses. Firms undertake investments in their own businesses when the potential cash flows or profits associated with these investments exceed alternative uses of cash.

HOW INVESTMENTS ARE FINANCED

Investments are funded from savings from one's income and borrowing from other people's savings, usually through the help of a financial intermediary such as a bank. The savings habits of households and firms influence the availability and cost of funds in the economy. Most people are uncomfortable with the risk of a sudden decline in their affordability or living standards; therefore, they have an incentive to save—to create some financial cushion to absorb unexpected shocks to their income. Shocks to income can arise from unemployment, disability, or costs associated with an expected future liability such as college tuition and related fees. For example, parents in a family with young children may want to put away a portion of their income to help cushion the effects of a potential risk of unemployment, to save towards affording a good education for their children, and to save up during years of employment in order to maintain their standard of living during retirement. Some forms of saving, such as contributing towards one's pension, are required by law. This legal saving requirement is aimed at avoiding a situation of having a large number of destitute senior citizens. For the most part, people make a conscious and voluntary decision to save toward particular objectives.

At any given point in time, individuals and firms with strong investment needs are unlikely to have the entire amount of financial resources needed to undertake these investments. A progressive economy finds efficient mechanisms to channel financial resources from people or entities that have excess income relative to their current consumption needs (the savers) to those with investment opportunities that require greater financial resources than is available from their current income and savings.

In the life cycle of an individual or firm, one has the potential to alternate between various stages of being a net provider of funds (a saver) and a net borrower or user of financial resources provided from the savings of other capital providers. For example, young people with a desire to invest in higher education are likely to become net users of funds when they borrow or obtain financial support from parents to finance the cost of their education. In early employment after graduation, they may become net providers of funds as their cost of living is likely to be low relative to their income. Their cost of living may rise (and their savings potential may decline) once they start families and need to pay for childcare. When a family decides to take a mortgage loan to buy a home, it becomes a net user of funds. The family may also want to save towards their children's education. By the time the children graduate from school and the couple pay off their mortgage loans, they may once again become net providers of capital (net savers). Firms often go through an investment phase to increase production or expand into new markets. The financial resources required to pursue these investment opportunities often exceed a firm's savings and profits. Many firms are only able to execute on investment opportunities by accessing funds from other capital providers. Over time, as these investments mature and generate revenue and profits to their potential, the earnings of the firm are likely to exceed its capital requirements, and the firm becomes a net provider of funds (by depositing excess cash in banks or purchasing financial securities).

To support sustainable investment activity, an economy needs to develop savings resources and mechanisms that help to efficiently and responsibly channel funds from savers to individuals and businesses with investment opportunities that require external funding. Developing a deep savings capacity in an economy is critical, because without creating policies that support saving practices and actual savings, there will be limited financial resources to support investments. If households and firms had to finance their investments (such as housing and business expansion) entirely from internally generated savings, some very large investments may never be undertaken or would take a very long time to execute. This would lead to structurally lower levels of investment activity in the economy, lower employment, and lower economic growth relative to its true potential.

In any economy that has a track record of price stability, interest rates rise when investment demand increases under favourable economic conditions, and they fall when investment demand weakens under frail economic conditions. Interest rates adjust upward or downward to match the amount of savings available to investment demands. The incentive to save increases when the return or interest to be earned rises (in real terms). Under favourable economic conditions, strong investment activity increases demand for capital and raises the level of interest rates in the economy. Falling appetite for investment, under weak and uncertain economic conditions, reduces demand for capital and lowers the level of interest rates in the economy.

Under strong economic conditions, employment, wages, and business prospects improve and households and firms have more confidence to undertake investments. Greater confidence in economic prospects entices households and firms to allocate capital away from low-risk investments such as bank deposits and government bonds into riskier assets such as stocks, real-estate and business expansion projects. The price of risky assets can rise sharply in periods of strong economic growth. As people allocate capital to riskier investments in search for higher returns, interest rates on bank deposits and government bonds rise to reflect the growing demand for capital. Rising interest rates make saving more attractive relative to current consumption and has the potential to increase the amount of funds available for investment. When economic conditions weaken, households and firms become less optimistic about employment prospects and investment returns. Capital providers allocate capital away from risky investments into lower-risk assets such as cash, bank deposits, and government bonds. This flight to safety (or quality) in an environment for lower investment demand, causes interest rates to fall.

In countries that have earned public trust in price stability, falling interest rates during an economic downturn and rising interest rates during favourable economic conditions help to deliver greater economic stability. Economic recovery in a downturn is supported by the low cost of funds, and rising interest rates during an economic boom help to cool-off investment activity by raising the cost of funds. This pattern of interest-rate movements helps to smooth economic cycles by making downturns less deep and not as long. The potential for excessive investment activity during periods of high confidence can also be curbed with the support of high interest rates.

THE ROLE OF FINANCIAL INTERMEDIARIES AND CAPITAL MARKETS

Financial intermediaries and capital markets efficiently channel funds from savers to borrowers and other users of funds. Financial intermediaries represent the interests of savers by allocating funds on their behalf, according to the risk and return preferences of the saver. Financial intermediaries employ investment professionals who have access to detailed information about the financial health and economic prospects of firms or individual borrowers and are better able to assess the risks associated with providing capital to such entities. Financial intermediaries pool the resources of savers together and allocate these savings to a wide variety of capital users. By playing a matching role between providers and users of capital, financial intermediaries enable savers to diversify risks beyond levels that savers could ever achieve on their own.

The market for providing financial intermediation services is highly competitive and there is a large reputation cost associated with practices that increase risks for savers. Financial institutions that abuse the interest of savers by taking excessive risks may end up losing their ability to attract capital or may lose their licence to operate in the industry. The economic incentives of financial intermediaries are generally aligned to the interests of capital providers. Profit prospects of financial intermediaries are tied to their ability to earn and maintain the trust of savers. Financial intermediaries that do a good job, by generating higher returns within the risk profiles chosen by capital providers, may attract a greater share of savings and ultimately earn more money for themselves.

Financial markets facilitate access to capital by creating standardized financial securities (such as stocks and bonds) that are actively traded. Individuals and businesses are more willing to provide capital when they have the flexibility to readily buy or sell securities. Financial intermediaries are the crucial link between financial markets and individual and business capital providers (savers). Capital markets (stock and bond markets) are a subsection of the financial markets that help to raise capital for long-term investment. Because of the need to maintain adequate cash resources to meet depositor requests, banks are mainly able to provide short-term funds with loan maturities extending to up to a few years only.

Bond markets provide an avenue for businesses and governments to borrow money for long periods. Stock markets provide firms with an opportunity to raise capital for long-term investment by selling fractional ownership units (shares) to people who are interested in directly participating in the financial prospects of a firm. Bonds are often sold with a fixed rate of interest. Bond prices and the eventual returns earned by bond investors can be affected by the prospects of a firm, but, because of the defined nature of regular interest payments, the link with a firm's economic prospects is weak. The financial returns on stocks are more closely linked to the economic prospects of a firm. Stock prices and stock returns are therefore much more volatile. Active trading in capital markets creates transparent and fair prices that transmit information about the economic prospects of the underlying firms. The ability to buy and sell financial securities at a fair price (i.e., without having an adverse impact on the price through one's purchase or sale actions) makes financial securities more marketable.

Financial markets and financial intermediaries play a crucial role in every economy. The failure of a major financial intermediary or financial market could break the public trust on which the whole financial system relies. The economic cost associated with a breakdown of the financial system can be large. Governments and firms may no longer have access to capital, and unemployment levels may rise due to restricted investment activity. To help preserve public trust and ensure the flow of capital from savers to borrowers, financial markets and financial intermediaries are regulated by independent public institutions, such as central banks, and dedicated regulatory bodies such as the Securities Exchange Commission in the United States and the Financial Services Authorities in the United Kingdom.

A key requirement of regulators is that shareholders (i.e., the owners) of financial intermediaries put up an adequate level of capital and be the first in line to absorb any losses before savers and other capital providers are put at risk. The minimum amount of shareholder capital required by regulators is linked to the size and quality of assets. Financial intermediaries may often need to raise additional capital when they are growing assets at a fast pace or when they are investing in more risky (and potentially more profitable) assets. Financial regulators monitor to ensure that financial intermediaries have adequate systems in place to keep track of funds and to prevent fraud. They also monitor to ensure that personnel who are involved in performing critical functions are adequately qualified and properly trained.

The financial compensation demanded by capital providers increases when the risk associated with an investment rises. Because the government cannot default on borrowings in its own currency, it is less risky to lend to the government than to lend to firms and individuals. The risk associated with lending to firms is lower than the risk associated with equity investments. As a result, capital providers demand higher financial compensation on equity investments (relative to interest rates on corporate bonds). Individuals and firms with strong economic prospects have greater access to funds at a lower cost than those with weaker economic prospects. Efficient financial markets are dynamic and promptly reflect available information about the economic prospects of government and businesses. The cost of borrowing for the government rises when savers and financial intermediaries acting on their behalf, become less confident about a government's economic policies or the sustainability of government spending plans. The cost of funds for individuals and firms rises when their financial prospects deteriorate and, at extreme levels, capital may become unavailable altogether when the associated risks become too high.

KEY FINANCIAL INTERMEDIARIES IN THE ECONOMY

BANKS take deposits from savers and lend to individuals, businesses, and governments. A bank generates revenue primarily through the interest it earns on consumer loans, such as mortgages, and loans to businesses. Banks also generate revenue from fees associated with other transactions. In addition to taking deposits and making loans, banks process payments on behalf of their customers and provide their customers with an opportunity to buy financial products such as portfolios of stocks and bonds. A bank pays depositors a portion of the interest it earns on loans. The bank spends the remainder of its revenue on wages, equipment, rent, and other services required to run its operations. Just like any other company, banks are set up to provide a service for customers and ultimately earn profits for their shareholders. Banks may only be able to distribute dividends to their shareholders when such payments do not threaten their ability to maintain adequate capital requirements set by regulators.

Who are your typical bank shareholders? In most countries, the cost of setting up a bank is too large for individual investors to fund on their own. Setting up a bank requires considerable financial resources to cover the minimum capital requirements set by regulators and expenses associated with opening bank branches, acquiring necessary equipment, and hiring qualified staff to manage the bank's operations. The minimum capital requirement is set in proportion to the size of a bank's assets. For example, if the minimum capital requirement is 10%, banks will be required to always maintain one dollar of capital for every ten dollars of loans (or assets). The requirement to maintain adequate levels of capital often means that a bank needs to raise additional capital in order to grow its business.

Due to the large amount of capital required to set up and expand operations, most banks raise capital on stock markets by selling shares to a very large number of individual and corporate capital providers. In countries with developed capital markets, workers and pensioners are collectively major shareholders in banks (and other firms listed on stock markets). However, individual workers who own tiny fractional shares may not be aware of which firms they own because financial intermediaries who manage pension funds (on behalf of individuals) typically do not provide that level of detail on pension holdings. The management of a bank represents the interest of bank customers (both depositors and borrowers) and a very large number of shareholders who typically each own tiny fractions of a bank's capital. In smaller economies, large international banks are able to set up local bank subsidiaries with their own capital and it may be more feasible for wealthy individuals and families to set up banks with their own capital.

Banks have limited ability to take financial risks. This is because depositors who provide the main source of funds for banks are primarily motivated by the safety of their savings than by the limited interest that banks pay on deposits. Because depositors may demand ready access to their money at any time, banks are required by regulators to maintain adequate levels of cash balances. Regulators monitor a bank's lending activities to ensure that the risk profile of bank loans is commensurate with the objectives of depositors. Because of their restricted ability to take risk, banks are only able to provide short-term funds for the most financially sound firms and individuals borrowers. For large loans, banks will typically require some form of collateral to help mitigate the risk to depositors in an event of default. For example, when a person takes a mortgage loan from a bank to buy a house, the house serves as collateral on the loan until the loan it is fully repaid. A bank may be able to take possession of the house (and sell it) when a mortgage holder is no longer able to honour the financial commitments on the loan.

Risks for depositors and shareholders in banks. In times of economic stress, business and wage prospects suffer, and there are fewer employment opportunities. In such an environment, a bank's assets and revenue are likely to come under stress because some businesses and individual borrowers may not be able to continue servicing their loans. When loans cannot be repaid or when borrowers miss interest payments, banks have to recognize the loss associated with bad loans. A bank's capital (which is provided by shareholders) is first in line to absorb losses from bad loans before depositors are put at risk. When losses eat into shareholder capital, the bank may need to raise additional capital to comply with minimum capital requirements. In extreme cases, losses from bad loans that cannot be repaid may exceed the amount of shareholder capital in the bank and depositors may face a meaningful risk of losing money.

Just like all other loan providers, financial compensation for depositors is limited to the interest they earn. However, depositors can end up losing a meaningful proportion of their savings in extreme cases when banks make large losses. In times of economic stress, the risk of depositors losing money has historically caused panic and bank runs (people queuing to withdraw all their savings out of fear that a bank may not be solvent enough to pay all depositors). In an effort to preserve public trust in banks and to reduce panic in times of economic stress, in many countries around the world, regulators have provided guarantees on deposits (a form of insurance on deposits) up to a certain amount. The savings potential in an economy and the ability of financial intermediaries to efficiently channel funds to meet the investment needs of households and firms are largely dependent on public trust in the stability of financial institutions.

Figure 10.1 shows a snapshot of a bank's balance sheet and the composition of a bank's assets and liabilities. One can see that the capital provided by shareholders of Standard Chartered Bank is only able to absorb a modest amount of losses on financial assets. Depositors (and other lenders) may stand to lose money when the value of loans and other assets fall by a modest amount (< 10%). $46 billion of shareholder capital is a substantial amount of money, but it is only able to absorb 7% of losses on assets. The limited capacity of shareholder capital to absorb losses reduces the risk profile of banks. It is possible to increase the safety of deposits by raising the minimum capital requirement. However, excessive increases in the minimum capital requirement of banks may reduce their ability to lend. Some banks may struggle to raise sufficient capital to meet high capital requirements and may have to close down. Regulators take extra measures to mitigate risk for depositors. These measures include placing restrictions on high-risk loans and tying the minimum capital requirement to the risk profile of a bank's loan portfolio. Banks that take greater risks in lending are required to put up additional shareholder capital.

Figure 10.1.

Standard Chartered Bank 2013 Balance Sheet Summary (in billions of US dollars)

Assets	$ bn	% of total	Liabilities and Shareholders Equity	$ bn	% of total
Cash and short term financial assets	84	12%	customer deposits	425	63%
loans to customers	373	55%	other bank borrowings	66	10%
debt and equity securities	102	15%	other financial liabilities	84	12%
other financial assets	62	9%	other liabilities	53	8%
All other assets (e.g property etc)	53	8%	Shareholders Equity	46	7%
Total Assets	674	100%	Total Liabilities + Shareholders Equity	674	100%

Source: Standard Chartered, Author

INSURANCE COMPANIES provide financial compensation to support people in times of unexpected events that can cause considerable financial loss. In order to benefit from such compensation, individuals and businesses need to purchase insurance contracts (or pay insurance premiums). Insurance contracts specify the period over which the insured qualify for receiving financial compensation in the event of loss. Purchasing insurance is a form of saving, because it provides financial support in times of unexpected loss and helps to preserve living standards. By diversifying the risk of a particular loss across a large number of customers, insurance companies are able to offer protection for relatively small cash premiums that are affordable for many buyers. For example, in a very large pool of drivers, the actual number of people involved in car accidents is much more predictable and small in relation to the size of the pool. Insurance companies invest cash premiums in liquid and low risk financial securities in order to have the flexibility to pay out specified cash compensation in times of loss or disaster. People purchase insurance against risks such as car accidents (auto insurance), personal injury or sickness (healthcare insurance), the unexpected death of a key income-earner in a family (life insurance), and property damage from fire and natural disaster (property insurance).

PENSION FUNDS receive and invest pension contributions from employees with the purpose of paying regular income to workers when they retire. In most countries, there is a legal requirement for all workers to make regular pension contributions. Pension funds pool together the pension contributions of a large number of workers. The greater scale makes it more efficient to hire qualified investment professionals to manage the funds directly or to delegate the fund management to a number of qualified investment firms. The long period of contributions during active employment (contributions can last over thirty years) and the predictability of the retirement age of contributors make it possible for pension funds to provide financial resources for long-term investments.

Pension funds play a considerable role in stock and bond markets because of their long-term investment horizon. Typically both employees and employers contribute towards pension savings. Pensions are designed to preserve affordability levels or living standards of retired people. Inflation wipes out the purchasing power of money and can erode living standards of retired people (who are less able to supplement their income with other jobs). In a number of countries some pension payments are linked to inflation rates to preserve the purchasing power of retirees. There are two main types of pension plans that employees can contribute into: defined-benefit and defined-contribution plans.

Defined-Benefit plans pay a regular retirement benefit (income) based on a formula rather than on returns associated with an employee's contributions. Under this plan, pension income is typically based on a retiree's final salary, number of years of employment, retirement age, and other factors. The pension-plan provider in a defined-benefit plan is typically one's employer or the government. In some countries, contributions to public pension schemes run by the government are mandatory for all employees. In countries that are dominated by private pension schemes, the government typically remains the primary pension provider for public sector employees. Under defined-benefit pensions, the plan provider, rather than the ultimate beneficiary (i.e., the employee), bears most of the financial risks associated with the pension plans. The plan provider bears the investment risk embedded with pension assets. Another key risk for the plan provider is the uncertainty associated with the mortality of the retiree. The plan provider faces great uncertainty over the number of years of pension benefit that has to be paid to an employee in retirement. It is very difficult to predict how long people are going to live (i.e., when pension payments will stop), and, because life expectancy is increasing over time, initial assumptions made about how long employees will live and the appropriate level of funds they require in retirement may not be accurate. The security of a retiree receiving pension payments under a defined-benefit plan depends on the financial health of the provider and the value of investments in the plan in relation to the size of pension liabilities. Retiree pension income is most secure when pension contributions have been prudently invested and earned attractive returns over time, to ensure that, the value of pension assets matches that of future pension commitments.

Many national (i.e., government controlled) defined-benefit pension schemes are under-funded; the value of pension assets is inadequate when compared to the size of future pension commitments. Because pension assets are inadequate, pension income for current retirees may be partly paid out of contributions from current workers as well as tax revenue. Companies with underfunded pension plans may be required to make additional yearly contributions to plug the hole.

Under defined-benefit pension plans, because the plan provider (the employer or the government) bears most of the financial risk for their pensions, people on defined-benefit pension plans take less interest in following the financial prospects of their invested pension contributions or in monitoring to establish the capacity of pension-plan assets to pay for their expected retirement income. In situations where pension-plan assets do not cover expected pay-outs to retirees, the prospects for retiree pension income become closely tied to the economic prospects of the plan provider. Large underfunded pension plans may depress pension income for current and future retirees.

Defined-Contribution plans are individual pension savings and investment accounts into which regular monthly pension contributions are made. The employee is responsible for deciding how his contributions are invested and he bears the full financial risk of the plan. Because it is an individual account, it is possible for workers to check at any given point to see how much they have saved up towards their pensions. The value of pension assets at any given point, and the eventual pension income that individuals can receive in retirement will depend on their actual contributions, as well as, the investment returns earned on pension assets over time. Under defined-contribution pension plans, retiree income is not directly linked to the number of years of employment, retirement age, or final salaries. Because of the greater discretion in investment choices and the size of employee contributions, two individuals with the same job, same income, and similar years of employment may have quite different amounts of pension assets and pension income in retirement. Under a defined-contribution pension plan, once workers attain a legislated minimum age (e.g. 55 years in the UK), they have unrestricted access to their entire pension assets. Defined-contribution plans require far greater responsibility and financial knowledge from employees. Under defined-contribution plans, workers are in greater control over their pension investments. Workers have greater knowledge about the size of their pension assets and the potential retirement income that they can draw from these assets. Their future pension income is less dependent on the economic prospects of their current employer or the government. Defined-contribution plans are becoming more popular with employers because they off-load long-term financial risks (from both investment performance and uncertainty around mortality) to employees. In many developing countries, governments remain the primary pension providers and defined contribution plans are more limited.

INVESTMENT FIRMS allocate funds on behalf of capital providers and other financial intermediaries. These firms hire investment professionals who earn fees by managing funds according to the risk and return preferences of their customers. Investment firms that generate a higher return within the risk preferences set by capital providers are likely to earn higher fees as they attract more assets from their clients. The professional investment services industry is highly competitive, and firms that do a poor job may lose assets and fees from their customers.

INVESTMENT BANKS help companies to raise long-term funds (both debt and equity) in capital markets in return for a fee. Investment banks put their reputation and capital at stake whenever they attempt to raise capital for a company. When a firm raises capital by providing information that turns out to be misleading, the investment bank that supported the firm to raise capital may suffer extensive reputational damage that can compromise its ability to operate. In order to create further incentives to earn the trust of investors, investment banks typically pledge their own financial resources to support firms who are trying to raise capital. The high reputational cost associated with investment banking activities helps to build public trust and facilitates access to long-term capital.

Most businesses are started with the financial resources of founders and their close associates. As a business grows, its capital requirements are likely to exceed the financial resources of founders and their close network of family and friends. At this stage businesses typically turn to banks for short-term funding. In order to finance long-term investments and rapid growth, businesses require long-term capital. Investment banks work with businesses to understand their capital needs and help them raise both debt and equity capital. In addition to helping to raise debt-funding by selling medium to long term bonds and equity-funding by selling fractional ownership stakes in a company (shares), investment banks provide a critical service by trading financial securities among each other and with other financial intermediaries to provide fair prices to buyers and sellers. The financial circumstances of investors are subject to change, and potential buyers of a financial security are more likely to purchase it if they know they will be able to sell these securities at a fair price at any time in the future.

PRIVATE-EQUITY FIRMS invest funds on behalf of wealthy individuals who have the capacity to lock away large amounts of money for an extended period of time. Unlike stocks and bonds, private-equity investments do not offer liquidity and cannot be readily sold at any time. Private-equity firms often invest in companies with a long-term horizon (five to ten years) and aim to realize attractive returns by working closely with company management to influence the strategic direction of firms. Private-equity funds take large ownership stakes in a few firms and provide low levels of diversification when compared with what one can achieve by buying a portfolio of stocks and bonds. Where possible, private-equity firms aim to enhance the returns of their investors by borrowing large amounts of money to fund investments in companies.

OTHER NON-BANK FINANCE COMPANIES are engaged in leasing, consumer finance, equipment finance, and so forth. These companies are similar to banks in their lending practices and assets, but unlike banks, which are mainly funded by customer deposits, non-bank finance companies raise funds from capital markets. They tend to concentrate on particular types of assets or loans and often take higher risks than banks.

*****

Investment options available to capital providers (corporate and individual savers) and financial intermediaries include cash, bank deposits, government-debt instruments, corporate bonds (loans made to companies), individual stocks (fractional ownership units in companies), collective investment funds (managed by professional investors and sold to the public) that allow access to a diverse portfolio of investments at a low cost, real estate, life insurance policies, private-equity funds, and others. Each investment options have unique risk characteristics. For example, cash and bank deposits are low risk investments because there is greater certainty over the value of one's savings. On the other hand, the value of stocks move up and down on a daily basis as new information about companies' prospects is incorporated into stock prices. Real-estate prices may move up and down over time. Assessing the value of real-estate may become challenging in an environment of limited transactions. Investment options that carry higher risks may provide a more attractive financial return over the long term.

Savers who allocate capital into bank deposits and debt instruments (government and corporate bonds) may be most vulnerable to the effects of inflation wiping out their purchasing power. The financial returns on debt and deposits are often limited to predetermined interest payments. When the rate of price increases in the economy exceeds the level of interest rates on bonds or deposits, the purchasing power of these capital providers can be depleted over time. Because of the potential of high inflation to erode the purchasing power of savers, countries that lack a strong track record of maintaining stable prices often have structurally low savings rates and high interest rates. Structurally low savings rates stifle investment activity and the development of financial markets.

How Capital Providers Allocate Their Savings.

The suitability of an investment option for individual or corporate savers depends on their time horizons—how long the savers plan to put money away—and their ability to bear the risk of financial loss or uncertainty in the value of their investments. Because current consumption is desirable and financial risk (the potential for losses or uncertainty in the value of investments) is undesirable, savers need to be compensated with a higher potential return in order to allocate capital to risky, and long-term assets such as stocks. Individuals and firms may put away various buckets of money to meet different financial needs, depending on the flexibility and urgency of the need. The different buckets of savings are each invested in appropriate financial instruments according to the savers' risk profiles. For example, a young family may be conservative with savings and allocate any excess capital to low-risk bank deposits or government bonds in order to save up to buy a house. The same family may be more aggressive in its pension allocations (a defined-contribution plan allows great discretion over investment choices), and invest pension assets in a diversified portfolio of stocks. Even though the value of stocks is more uncertain than bank deposits in the short term, stocks may be more suitable investments for the family's pension savings, because these savings have a long time horizon and can only be withdrawn upon retirement. Because of the long time horizon associated with pension contributions, the family is willing to embrace higher uncertainty in the daily value of stock investments in exchange for a higher potential return by the time they retire. Despite the potential for higher returns, the family is unlikely to allocate savings earmarked for buying a family home into stocks, because these savings need to be readily accessible in the short term. For individuals who have defined-contribution pension plans and employers or the government who manage defined benefit pension assets, the suitability of investment choices for a pension plan changes over time, to reflect changing liquidity needs of workers. The risk profile of pension plan assets becomes more moderate as the average age of beneficiaries increases. A pension portfolio that is heavily invested in stocks may be suitable for young workers but as they approach retirement age, lower risk investment such as government bonds, may become more appropriate.

REAL-ESTATE OWNERSHIP AND THE IMPACT OF DEBT FINANCING ON INVESTMENT RISK AND RETURNS.

Many people own a house or property during their lifetime. In countries that pursue prudent economic policies and embrace monetary integrity, property ownership is more feasible because of the availability of low-interest mortgage loans from banks to buy houses. Typically a person can buy a house by contributing a small fraction (10% to 30%) of the total value and borrowing the remainder from a bank. Home buyers who take mortgage loans from banks are required to make monthly payments until they repay the loans in full. These monthly payments consist of interest on the loan and partial repayment of the loan principal.

When people buy property (or any other assets) with the help of loans, even though they may have directly contributed only a fraction of the actual cost of the house, they own the economic rights to the property; they stand to profit if house prices go up and lose if house prices fall. However, their economic interests are only partial because they are still associated with liabilities—the required monthly payments to loan providers until the loans are repaid in full. Banks and other mortgage-loan providers have the right to take ownership of houses if interest and principal payments are not forthcoming. It is only when one completely pays off a mortgage loan that one can claim to own a house in full (i.e., without any associated liability). On a more technical level, a person who buys a house with the help of a mortgage loan only owns the equity in the house rather than the whole house. The value of the equity is equal to the current market value of the house minus the outstanding mortgage loan (a liability).

When house prices rise, the value of homeowners' equity can increase tremendously, and the return on their investments could be significantly larger than if they were to own the house in full (without the help of a loan). People who buy houses with the help of mortgage loans have the potential to benefit to the full extent of price increases on the whole house even though they only invested a fraction of the cost. For example, when a person contributes $30,000 of cash and borrows $70,000 to buy a $100,000 home and house prices rise by 20 percent, the value of the house increases by $20,000 to $120,000 and the value of his equity increases to $50,000 (i.e., the current house price of $120,000 minus mortgage loans of $70,000). This represents a 67 percent return on his initial investment (i.e., a $20,000 gain in equity value vs the initial cash investment of $30,000). If he were to own the house in full by paying $100,000 in cash, the return on his investment from the price increase will only be 20 percent (i.e., a $20,000 gain in equity value vs the initial cash investment of $100,000)

Rising interest rates (on outstanding mortgage loans) and falling house prices are major risks for homeowners. Unless interest rates on mortgage loans are fixed for long periods, changes in interest rates can represent a substantial source of risk for homeowners. When inflation risk in the economy rises, interest rates can increase sharply. In an environment of high interest rates, new homeowners may shy away from taking mortgage loans, but existing homeowners will be faced with substantially higher monthly loan-servicing requirements. At any given point, if a homeowner were to sell the house, he or she would be required to repay the bank in full before accessing the remaining proceeds (if there are any).

The equity that a homeowner has invested in a house can be wiped out when house prices fall sharply. In extreme cases, homeowners may have to contribute additional financial resources to sell a house when the equity value is no longer sufficient to absorb losses. Following from the previous example, if house prices were to fall by 20 percent, the value of the house will fall to $80,000. After deduction the value of mortgage loans, the value of a homeowner's equity will fall to $10,000 (i.e. current house price of $80,000 minus the outstanding mortgage loan of $70,000). The homeowner's return (if he or she were to sell the house) will now be a loss of 67 percent on the initial $30,000 cash investment (i.e., a loss of $20,000 on his initial investment). If the house had been entirely purchased in cash (i.e., no mortgage loans), the loss on the initial investment would be 20 percent ($20,000 loss on an initial investment of $100,000). When house prices fall by more than 30 percent, the homeowner with the mortgage no longer has any equity in the house (actually, there is negative equity value) and he may be forced to put up additional capital before he can sell the house. It is important to note that both losses and gains from changes in house prices can only be realized when houses are sold (i.e., loans have to be immediately repaid in full upon sale).

Debt financing of assets has the potential to magnify profits and losses. When firms employ large amounts of debt to finance investments, this can magnify potential gains and losses and may increase the risk of bankruptcy (i.e., the inability to generate sufficient cash flows for interest and debt payments). The potential financial loss on a mortgage-financed home is not limited to the amount that the homeowner has invested in the house. Because real estate can be easily financed with loans from banks, misconceptions about risks associated with ownership are more applicable to real estate than to other investment products. For the most part, banks do not lend to households to invest in stocks, bonds, and other financial securities. Typically, when people buy other financial securities, they own complete economic rights without taking on any external liability. Their financial loss is limited to the amount of money they invested in these securities.

IMPACT OF GOVERNMENT POLICIES ON CAPITAL MARKETS. Government borrowing requirements are often the largest in the market for funds and forms the benchmark upon which other credit markets (e.g., mortgages and corporate borrowing) develop. The government's management of the value of money and the economy has a significant influence on the savings habits of individuals and companies. The government's spending habits and borrowing requirements have the ability to soak up a significant proportion of available savings resources in a country. When the government undertakes large spending plans and finances them with a considerable amount of borrowing, it may soak up most of the savings capacity in the economy and drive interest rates to high levels. Excessive borrowing requirements restrict the ability of individuals and businesses to borrow. When interest rates on government risk-free borrowings are high, savers may have less interest in providing long-term capital for businesses.

GLOBALIZATION OF FINANCIAL MARKETS. Growing economic interaction between nations extends beyond consumer products and includes access to capital and investment opportunities. Many large corporations operate businesses across several countries and are able to access capital from all over the world. Financial intermediaries, in countries that have well developed capital markets, provide reliable and cost-efficient platforms that enable individual and corporate savers to allocate capital across a wide range of international investment opportunities. Globalization can enable a more efficient allocation of resources, because it allows companies to capitalize on the most promising investment opportunities on a global scale, supported by the most favourable sources of funds. Globalization of financial markets allows for a deeper level of diversification of savings to enhance returns and to protect capital providers from economic and political shocks in a particular country.

Investing in foreign financial assets carries additional risks. Currency fluctuations and policy initiatives of foreign governments can have a significant impact on the value of foreign investments. Even though investing in government bonds in one's home country is considered a low-risk investment, investing in bonds issued by foreign governments may present substantially higher risks. Typically, capital will flow from countries with excess savings resources in order to seek higher returns in countries that have insufficient capital to finance attractive investment opportunities.

FIGURE 10.2.

Nestle Shareholder Base (2013)

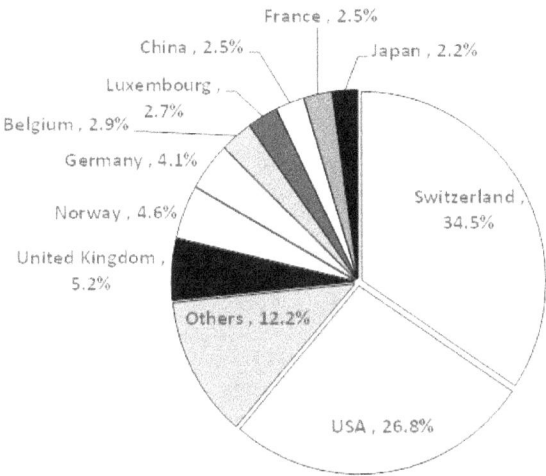

SOURCE: NESTLE, AUTHOR

In countries that have a strong savings culture often built over a long period of time on the back of a track record of prudent government policies, interest rates (the cost of funds) fall in times of low economic growth and weak investment demand. Under these conditions, capital is more likely to seek higher returns with governments and companies in foreign countries that are still experiencing strong demand growth. In periods of strong economic growth, the flow of international funds into a country may help to increase funding resources and lower funding costs for businesses and the government while also strengthening the value of the country's currency.

For capital providers, the relative appeal of foreign investments may decline when economic conditions in the home country start to improve or when economic prospects in the foreign country become less favourable. When economic conditions at home start to improve, domestic interest rates, stock prices, and other asset prices rise to reflect the favourable economic outlook. When investors withdraw capital from a foreign country in order to participate in improved opportunities at home, the value of financial securities in the foreign country is likely to fall and its currency may weaken partly because international investors are both selling down these assets and taking their capital out of the country. Due to the impact of the flow of funds on asset prices and currencies, investments in foreign financial assets, including bonds issued by foreign governments, can be more risky when compared to domestic investments.

The cost of capital is likely to be high in societies that consume most of their income and save little. When people enjoy a high level of satisfaction from immediate consumption, they require higher financial compensation to induce them to save. The appetite for saving may have some cultural influences. However, a government's track record on price and economic stability can have a considerable impact on the willingness of citizens to save. Countries with high levels of inflation often have low savings rates. High inflation creates an environment of high interest rates, higher levels of economic uncertainty and low levels of investment. Prudent government policy can improve savings habits. A good starting point will be the delivery of a long track record of price stability. Other policies that may support saving behaviour when there is a stable price outlook include tax incentives to save towards retirement, children's education, or healthcare; and the privatization of pension funds.

THE EMERGING-MARKETS INTEREST-RATE PUZZLE: Rising interest rates under deteriorating economic conditions.

Contrary to intuitive expectations, interest rates in a number of developing countries tend to rise in periods of weak economic growth and fall in times of favourable economic conditions. The movement of interest rates in these countries creates greater economic instability by raising the cost of borrowing in a downturn and easing the cost of borrowing and access to capital in times of great confidence.

A number of developing countries have structurally low savings rates because governments and central banks have historically abused public confidence by printing money to finance government spending, and the resulting erosion in the value of money makes saving less attractive for citizens. Governments that are too reliant on money-supply growth to stimulate the economy (rather than productivity initiatives) create an environment of high price increases, a low saving culture, and high interest rates. Because of their low savings rates, governments and businesses in many developing countries become reliant on foreign capital providers to fund investments.

Rising (domestic and foreign) investor confidence during periods of strong economic growth increases the availability of capital to governments and businesses in these countries. The rising supply of capital may help to lower the level of interest rates during favourable economic conditions. High investor confidence in periods of strong economic growth also makes foreign investors less sensitive to the higher risks associated with such investments. A greater supply of capital, lower interest rates, and improving government finances increase the willingness of governments to pursue prudent policies, which further boosts the confidence of domestic and foreign capital providers.

Historical evidence in a number of these countries suggests that under weak economic conditions, governments become less committed to policy integrity and may have stronger incentives to initiate policies that create illusion of gain in the short term. When economic conditions weaken, all capital providers (both foreign and domestic) become less focused on opportunities for high returns and more sensitive to the higher-risk profile of these investments and increased policy uncertainty.

Historically, in periods when economic conditions and government finances deteriorate, some governments have intervened to weaken investor confidence by funding a large proportion of government spending through the printing of money (essentially an additional tax in weak economic conditions) and excessive borrowing. These actions drive interest rates to elevated levels. In extreme cases, governments have intervened in key sectors of the economy to lower the cost of services to customers by arbitrarily freezing or lowering utility tariffs, setting price controls on consumer goods, freezing interest rates on bank lending, and restricting access to foreign currency. Such governments lose credibility in the eyes of foreign and domestic capital providers. Foreign capital providers respond to these heightened risks by selling their investments and repatriating funds back to their home countries (a flight to quality or safety). In fear of losing the purchasing power of their savings, domestic investors channel their capital into buying durable goods in the local economy or buying international assets (or currencies) where possible. As foreign and domestic investors withdraw capital, interest rates rise to compensate for the heightened risks in the economy.

Particularly in countries with large savings deficits, the strong inflows of foreign capital in periods of strong economic growth and rapid outflows in periods of weakening economic prospects, can amplify opportunities in good times and increase uncertainty in bad times. This pattern tends to make such economies more unstable relative to countries that rely on more sustainable sources of capital. Another way to interpret the risk of international capital flows is that countries that are interested in attracting foreign capital need to maintain a high level of policy integrity through the cycle. The advantages of tapping into a global capital pool are only sustainable with the delivery of a long track record of policy integrity. Developing countries that have structurally improved the integrity of their policy framework over long periods of time have been rewarded with access to more sustainable sources of international capital.

11

FINANCIAL MARKETS AND ECONOMIC GROWTH

Financial markets support greater economic participation among citizens and promote higher levels of economic engagement. In addition to mobilizing large financial resources for investment, financial markets have the potential to support productivity gains in the economy. Financial markets generate transparent and independent assessment of resource allocation initiatives and provide valuable information that can lead to a more efficient utilization of a country's resources. Stock markets in particular are instrumental in helping companies raise large amounts of capital for long-term investment. Many investment opportunities in the economy are long term in nature and need to be appropriately funded with long-term capital. In the absence of a well-developed stock market, many potentially attractive investment opportunities may not be realized.

Well-functioning financial markets help to democratize investment opportunities among the population. At the very minimum, many individuals and households would own investments such as bank deposits, property and/or pension fund investments. The value of these investments is likely to benefit from government policies that support sustainable economic growth. In countries where opportunities to invest in financial assets are readily accessible by the average household, there is greater ownership of financial assets by a broad segment of the population. Broad ownership of financial assets creates strong incentives for ordinary citizens to monitor government policies and support policies that are more likely to deliver sustainable economic growth. For example, mass ignorance about the relationship between interest rates and inflation may be more common in countries where structurally poor economic policies have discouraged people from saving and where most people do not have bank accounts or mortgage loans. On the other hand, in countries that have delivered a long track record of prudent economic policies, most households are active capital providers (savers in pensions, bank accounts, etc.) or active capital consumers (who take mortgage loans, education loans, consumer loans, etc.) at different stages.

In countries where there is a high level of participation in financial markets, households are more likely to readily and transparently see the impact of policy changes on the value of their financial assets and liabilities. This creates deeper incentives within the population to safeguard governance standards. When a typical household has an economic stake in government securities and shares in a wide range of businesses (e.g., through pension assets), it becomes more sensitive to policy changes that have an adverse impact on the economy. Poor economic policies may have a negative impact on the value of financial assets and household wealth. The typical household is therefore better incentivized to "police" government policy on a regular basis or, at the very least, become more active in discouraging specific government policies that negatively impact the value of savings or wealth on a structural basis. Since government policies are meant to enhance the well-being of people, having this objective and transparent feedback mechanism can support higher governance standards.

Financial markets generate significant amounts of information about economic prospects in a country. Interest-rate movements may provide information about the potential impact of government economic policies. Share-price movements may provide more objective information about economic prospects for businesses in the economy. Differences in the share price performance of companies within the same industry can provide information about the quality of management and of capital-allocations decisions. The disclosure of regular financial information about a firm's business prospects, industry conditions, competitive environment, input costs, profitability, and global cost competitiveness may be useful for all stakeholders (governments, employees, competitors, shareholders, banks, regulators, etc.) in making more informed economic decisions. A considerable amount of financial-market information is freely accessible from company annual reports, websites of central banks, and specialist finance sites such as Bloomberg, Google Finance and Reuters.

Financial markets support sustainable economic growth by allocating greater capital resources to firms that create economic value. There are many investment opportunities in the economy, but some have the potential to create more value than others. Because resources (including capital resources) are limited in any economy, not all investment opportunities can be realized. It is therefore essential to develop a framework for allocating resources to opportunities that create the most value for society. Financial markets provide an avenue for independently assessing the attractions of investment opportunities. Well-functioning financial markets enable a highly democratized assessment and capital allocation process which cannot be "captured" by any interested party over a considerable period. Financial markets create a merit-based incentive system that promotes economic value creation. Firms, managers, and employees that create substantial economic value for society are rewarded with greater capital resources to deliver more value in the future.

INTEGRITY AND PUBLIC TRUST ARE INTEGRAL TO THE DEVELOPMENT OF FINANCIAL MARKETS.

Without a broad level of public trust in government policies to ensure price stability, people are more likely to consume their income than save, and, even when they save, they are less likely to provide capital for long-term investments. Without trust in the solvency of banks and public trust that depositors can readily access their funds, it would not be possible for many businesses and individuals to access bank loans. Unless capital providers have confidence in the reliability of financial information that firms report, savers will be unlikely to take up opportunities to become long-term capital providers (e.g., by buying shares in companies). Functioning financial markets are invaluable to economic progress and economic stability. To preserve their crucial role, financial markets and financial intermediaries are heavily regulated to promote integrity and public confidence. Public trust can be costly to restore after it has been broken.

WHAT MAKES AN INVESTMENT OPPORTUNITY ECONOMICALLY VIABLE OR ATTRACTIVE?

Investments require the spending of capital and other resources in the short-term and offer the potential to generate profits (or cash flows) in the future. In order to be sustainable, an investment or a business needs to generate enough revenue to pay for the cost of resources employed in production. Capital is a key resource employed in the production of goods and services, and capital providers require adequate financial compensation. Capital providers are often the last in line to receive financial compensation, because unlike other resources employed in production such as raw materials or labour, the amount of capital employed (e.g. in factory machinery) is more permanent in nature and not so dependent on daily production rates.

Creating economic value means that a firm would generate a profit after paying a fair compensation for all the resources employed to conduct its business, including a fair compensation for capital. In any economic activity, value is created when the revenue generated is greater than the costs of all resources employed in delivering a product or a service. For an investment to be economically viable, it has to generate sufficient revenue to pay for all operating costs such as raw-material costs, employee salaries, and so forth; pay taxes to the government; and have sufficient underlying profits or cash flows to adequately remunerate capital providers. In other words, for a business or an investment to generate economic value, the return on capital (i.e., the ratio of underlying profits to the amount of capital invested in the business) has to be greater than the cost of capital for that business. The cost of capital for a business is the level of financial compensation or financial return that providers of capital demand for investing in the business. When the underlying level of profits or cash flows is not sufficient to pay an adequate compensation for the use of capital, the business is failing to create economic value, and capital providers will have less appetite for supplying funds for future investment in the business. The financial compensation demanded by capital providers depends on the length of time they are required to provide capital and the risks associated with the investments. The cost of capital rises when the risk profile of an investment increases and capital is required for longer periods.

STOCK MARKETS AND ECONOMIC GROWTH

Stock markets provide an important source of long-term capital for firms. The ability of companies to borrow to finance investments is restricted. Lenders have a limited capacity to take on large risks and typically do not provide long-term capital. When businesses have attractive growth opportunities and require large amounts of capital to finance long-term investment, a well-functioning stock market is the most reliable and efficient source of capital. Stock markets allow a wide variety of investors to buy fractional units of ownership in companies. Their ownership presents them with opportunities to earn financial rewards that are linked to the profit-growth prospects of these companies.

Owning a large proportion of shares in one company (e.g. a typical entrepreneur or family business owner) may be too risky for many capital providers. The opportunity to buy fractional units of ownership in several companies allows for high levels of investor diversification and lowers the cost of capital for businesses. Individuals or households with small amounts of capital are able to buy shares in several companies or buy funds that provide even greater diversification across a much large number of businesses. Well-developed stock markets have a large number of buyers and sellers of shares at any given point. This creates fair and transparent prices that improve the marketability of shares for both investors and companies. By creating efficient access to ownership stakes in a diverse range of companies, stock markets allow individuals, households, and businesses to take greater ownership in the economic prospects of a country. The profit potential of firms is often tied to the economic prospects of a country, and high levels of stock ownership within a country can inspire people to take greater interest in economic issues and support policies that are more likely to deliver sustainable economic growth.

Compared to lower-risk investments such as bank deposits, government bonds and corporate bonds, the value of company shares is more volatile. Over short periods of time, stock prices can move up or down by large amounts, a feature that is undesirable for capital providers with a short-term horizon. However, because the stock market essentially provides an ownership stake in the economic prospects of a country, over long periods of time, stock prices are likely to rise in value, supported by growth in the economy. Through the stock market, capital providers with a long-term investment horizon have an opportunity to make more attractive financial returns while supporting greater investment and economic growth in their respective countries.

Stock markets support the efficient allocation of resources by providing greater access to capital for companies that create economic value. Companies that create sustainable economic value are more likely to be rewarded with rising share prices and a high valuation relative to profits or other company metrics. Rising share prices for good capital allocators increase access to capital at more affordable rates. The share price and valuation of businesses that do not generate sustainable economic value are more likely to fall or remain low. Share prices fall because of weakening prospects for profit-growth and low levels of investor confidence in the ability of a company and its management to create economic value. Capital providers are less willing to provide funds for companies that are not generating sufficient profits to pay a fair compensation for the use of capital.

By rewarding companies that create economic value with greater capital resources and withdrawing capital from firms that do not generate sufficient revenue to cover their cost of production, stock markets send strong and independent signals that help an economy to allocate capital resources more efficiently.

Share prices change every day to reflect the most current information about the profit prospects of a company. When the management of companies heed the signals contained in share-price movements and improve their capital allocation practices, firms and their shareholders as well as the economy in general, may reap positive rewards in the long-term. Companies that sustain high valuation ratios over long periods send powerful signals about the principles behind sustainable value creation. A firm would command a higher than average valuation ratio (e.g., a higher than average price to earnings ratio) when investors are optimistic about the potential for the company to generate higher than average profit growth from ongoing investments in products and services. For example, innovative companies that deliver desirable products at compelling prices usually command high valuation ratios because of superior prospects for revenue and profit growth. Information contained in valuation ratios can be useful for competitors, other businesses, entrepreneurs, and other stakeholders, and it may help to improve the overall allocation of capital resources to enhance value creation in the economy.

Stock markets enable capital providers to efficiently diversify their investments. Greater opportunities for diversification supports economic stability. Many capital providers derive their income or wealth from their primary economic activities. The income and capital prospects of employees are often tied to that of their employer. The economic prospects of a firm is often tied to opportunities and risks in its industry. Without attractive opportunities for diversification, capital providers may not invest efficiently. With limited opportunities for external investments, firms may be pressured to re-invest any excess capital in their own businesses. Households may be forced to invest excess income in a limited number of accessible opportunities such as real-estate. When capital is concentrated in a limited number of investments, capital providers may become vulnerable to drastic changes in the prospects of one sector of the economy. For example, when all the excess income of a household is tied-up in real-estate investments, the financial stability of the household may be compromised in an environment of falling house prices. Well-developed stock markets provide an attractive opportunity for diversification that offer better protection against adverse changes in the conditions of any one industry. Stock markets provide an opportunity to diversify sources of income away from a primary employer or an industry and can support greater stability in the financial prospects of households and firms. The greater liquidity in stock market investments provides flexibility for capital providers to optimize their capital allocation decisions under different circumstances. Unlike other investments, it is more efficient to sell small amounts of shares to finance specific capital needs that may arise in the future.

Stock markets allow for the separation of firms' ownership from management. The arm's-length relationship between the two, makes it possible to improve management practices across firms and the economy in general. Shareholders set incentives for managers and have objective standards (ultimately in the form of share-price movements) for reviewing management initiatives. Managers who create value for shareholders are more likely to keep their jobs and earn large financial rewards, and those who destroy shareholder capital are more likely to be voted out. The arm's-length relationship between owners and managers creates stronger incentives for managers to allocate capital efficiently. The separation of ownership and management also helps to mobilize resources from a larger number of capital providers who do not have the skills, time, or interest in managing firms directly. The separation of ownership and management makes it possible for businesses to transition through generations, so long as, they maintain their ability to create sustainable economic value.

Stock markets provide a low-cost opportunity for investors with small amounts of capital to gain exposure to key sectors of the economy. For example, it may be more feasible for individuals with small amounts of capital to express their optimism about real-estate prospects by buying shares in a property developer than buying a real property that requires far greater sums of capital. Investors that form a favourable view on agricultural commodities may find it more efficient to buy shares in companies that grow crops or produce fertilizer, tractors, and other agricultural inputs than invest directly in farmlands to produce crops. For people captivated by the transformational potential of new technology and innovations, the stock market provides a low-cost opportunity to gain exposure to a large number of firms involved in the frontier of research and development across many fields. Workers who are optimistic about the economic prospects of their employer can transform this optimism into an economic stake at a low cost.

The ability to gain economic exposure to a large and diverse set of opportunities at a low cost, democratizes opportunities for investment among a population and can support stronger levels of economic awareness and higher governance standards.

Stock markets provide transparent, independent, and reliable valuation of firms, which improves access to capital. Independent valuation of companies helps capital providers to make informed investment decisions and increases access to capital. The relative valuation of a company compared to its annual profits (or some other metric) provides an objective and efficient basis to compare the attractiveness of investment opportunities across several companies in the same industry. The value of a company relative to its profits (price to earnings ratio or PE ratio) of typical stocks in the economy can often range from ten times to twenty times during an economic cycle. On a diverse portfolio of stocks, the ratio generally corresponds to the degree of optimism on the economic prospects of firms. Firms that have the potential to create a considerable amount of economic value as result of higher than average profit growth prospects tend to command a higher valuation ratio (e.g. PE ratio). When two firms that invest similar amounts of capital are expected to grow profits at comparable rates in the future, the firm that is able to generate more predictable profits will command a higher valuation ratio. Investors are prepared to pay up for lower levels of uncertainty in profit prospects.

The value of a business on the stock market reflects a transparent and independent assessment of value that investors place on profit or cash-flow prospects over the life cycle of a firm. The transparent valuation enables firms to raise long-term capital more efficiently. An independent valuation of a company also promotes greater access to debt financing. When loans are backed by assets that have a transparent valuation, loan providers feel more comfortable about the risks they are taking and are more likely to lend to companies at lower interest rates.

By allowing for greater diversification of risk for each investor and providing an efficient mechanism to pool resources from a large number of investors, stock markets can materially increase the scope of investment possibilities in an economy. Investments in a number of sectors such as technology, medical research, oil and gas, mining, electricity production and distribution and telecommunications require a considerable amount of capital. These investments may have immense potential for profit growth and create substantial value for society, but the considerable scale of resources required and the high risk profile creates a major challenge for funding investments in these industries. Some investments can only be enabled by a funding structure that spreads the enormous capital requirement as well as the investment risk among a large number of capital providers. By creating an efficient mechanism that pools resources from a large number of investors in a diversified manner (with each individual investor contributing only a small fraction of his capital to such high-potential but high-risk investments), stock markets enable investment in activities that may otherwise be left unfunded because of their high levels of risk. Some investment opportunities simply require too much capital for even the wealthiest individuals to fund on their own. By selling fractional ownership units to millions of shareholders, funding such large investments becomes more feasible. Through enabling a greater scope of investment initiatives, the diversification power of well-functioning stock markets can promote innovation and entrepreneurial zeal in an economy. Because they can own tiny fractions of many companies, shareholders themselves are typically diversified and better positioned to withstand unforeseen and extreme cases of financial loss in any one investment.

Stock markets provide an efficient mechanism that supports economic growth and investment activity by channeling long-term savings to finance long-term investments. However, unless governments undertake policies that support healthy savings behaviour and economic stability, the existence of a stock market in a country may not necessarily support investment activity. Stock markets are now present in many countries but some are not living up to their potential of mobilizing long-term capital for investment. The political and economic environment in which a stock market operates has an impact on its effectiveness in mobilizing capital. In countries where economic policy discourages saving, stock markets are less likely to be effective in mobilizing capital. In all countries, pension savings are a considerable source of long term capital. When the government has a monopoly over managing pension assets, stock markets may not function effectively because of the dominance of one capital provider. Stock markets may struggle to provide a truly democratized and independent assessment of economic value creation because one key player can dictate access to capital and the cost of capital for businesses. Stock market liquidity; the ability to buy and sell shares efficiently, has an impact on the willingness of the public to provide capital to firms with long-term investment opportunities. When a firm's capital is controlled by a few influential shareholders, the ability to buy and sell shares may be limited for many other investors. The ability of a few key shareholders to influence investment decisions may work against the interest of minority shareholders (i.e., members of the public). Capital providers value opportunities for diversification. When the stock market in a country has a limited number of companies or when firms on the stock market are largely exposed to a few sectors of the economy, the stock market may not offer an attractive diversification opportunity for capital providers. The provision and enforcement of effective laws that protect capital providers from abuse can be crucial in promoting access to capital in the stock market. In order for stock markets to maintain fairness and transparency, buyers and sellers of stocks can only make their investment decisions on publicly available information. When company insiders (founders, management, employees and their families or friends) take advantage of their preferential access to information to make a profit on stocks at the expense of the general public, the stock market's ability to mobilize capital can be highly compromised.

Case Study 11.1. Analyzing Returns to a Firm's Stakeholders with Company Financials Based on Nestlé's 2013 Annual Report

Nestlé is the largest food and beverage company in the world. It sells baby food, bottled water, breakfast cereals, food seasonings, ice cream and other dairy products, tea and coffee, and many other products in 196 countries, supported by production in 86 factories spread around the world. Nestlé's brands are easily recognized and include household names such as Nescafé, Kit Kat, and Maggi that generate over $1 billion dollars of sales every year.

Figure 11.1. Nestlé Global Sales Distribution (2013)

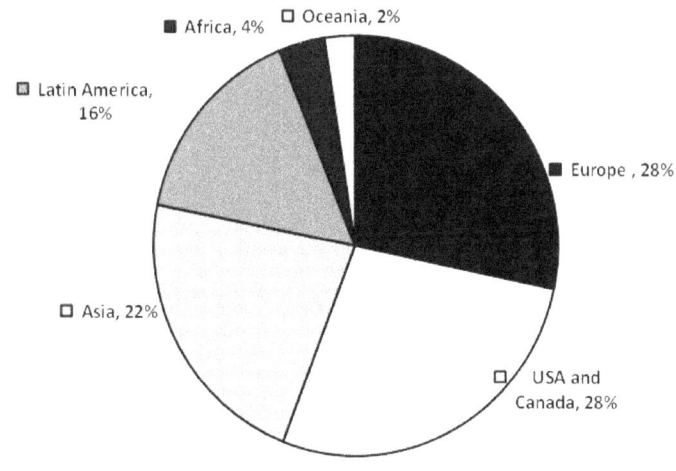

Source: Nestlé, Author

In 2013, Nestlé generated just over $100 billion in global sales. To generate this amount of sales, Nestlé spent about $87 billion on raw materials, manufacturing expenses, distribution expenses, advertising, and employee salaries. Nestlé uses raw materials such as milk, sugar, palm oil, coffee, cocoa, flavors, and plastics to formulate and package its products for sale. Nestlé large demand for raw materials creates a considerable number of jobs on sugar plantations in Brazil, cocoa farms in West Africa, coffee plantations in Ethiopia, palm plantations in many tropical countries, and dairy farms around the world.

In 2013, Nestlé directly employed 330,000 people in operations across 196 countries and paid $17 billion for employee compensation. This equates to an average employee compensation of $50,000 for the year. From their salaries, Nestle employees are able to support their households and local governments (by paying taxes on their income). Nestlé's marketing spend supports many jobs in marketing and advertising agencies in many countries. The global distribution of Nestlé products is made possible by the large number of small and medium-sized distributors and shop owners who act as intermediaries between Nestlé and the final consumer. In this way, Nestlé's products support a considerable number of income-earning opportunities around the world.

After deducting all expenses incurred in producing and selling products, Nestlé generated $14 billion in operating profit. From this amount, it paid interest on its borrowings (a cost of $700 million) and $3.6 billion in taxes to governments in the 196 countries where it sells products. This is a meaningful amount of tax revenue that supports governments around the world. Even though Nestlé was founded and remains headquartered in Switzerland, its global footprint requires it to pay taxes for profits generated in each country where it operates. In this way, globalization has the potential not only to create significant employment in other countries, but also adds to government revenue in these countries.

In many parts of the world, Nestlé invests locally in partnership with other organizations. Its share of income generated from such investment partnerships amounted to $1.4 billion dollars in 2013, and its total profit for the year amounted to $11.5 billion. Profits generated after paying all suppliers, employees, distribution and marketing services, interest on debt, and taxes, belong to Nestlé's shareholders, who provide a permanent source of capital for the company. From its annual profit, Nestle paid out almost $8 billion to shareholders mainly in the form of cash dividends (income). It also invested about $6 billion in capital expenditure to maintain and improve its asset base.

Who are the Nestlé shareholders who took home almost $8 billion of dividends in 2013? Are they all based in Switzerland? Globalization of capital markets provides opportunities for investors all over the world to become Nestlé shareholders. In 2013, the company had a market value of $230 billion. The shareholder base was diversified, and Swiss capital providers owned 34% of the company. The majority of shares are owned by financial intermediaries on behalf of pensioners and other capital providers from several countries. Even though the dividend payment is large in absolute terms, each individual shareholder receives dividends in relation to the amount he or she invested. In 2013, a shareholder who bought 1 share of Nestlé at an average price of $75 received a cash dividend of $2.5 (or 3.4% of his investment value). Nestlé shareholders provide long-term capital for developing or acquiring key brands, and financing assets that are permanent in nature such as factory buildings and equipment, distribution trucks and office buildings.

Figure 11.2. Distribution of Nestlé's Shareholder Base (2013)

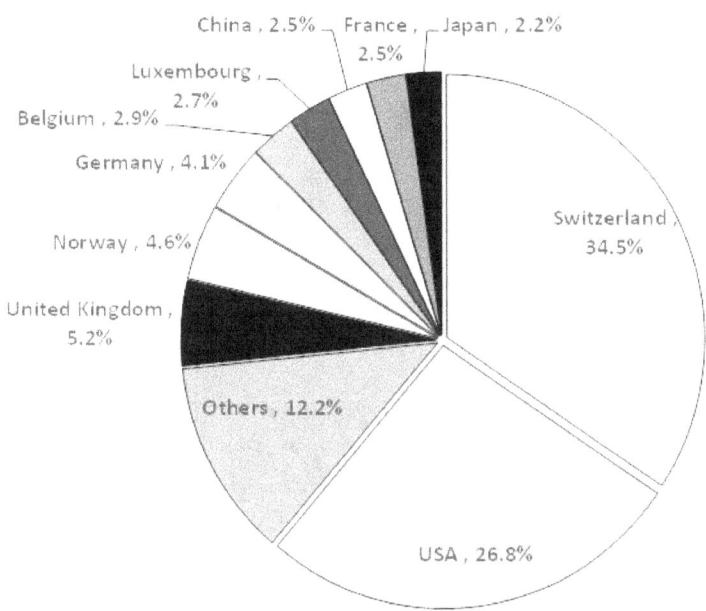

Source: Nestlé, Author

Does Nestlé create sustainable economic value? Should the company be encouraged to invest for growth? Nestlé's main assets are made up of equipment in factories, trucks for distribution, some raw material stocks needed to maintain production runs, and, most importantly, the value of its brands. Many other companies could afford to buy similar equipment from suppliers but may struggle to compete with Nestlé's products because the company has built and acquired strong brands over many years. Nestlé invests heavily in product innovation and advertising to create consumer awareness that associates Nestlé's brands with quality, desirable taste, and health. It is the strength of these brands that underpin Nestlé's high level of profitability.

For 2013, Nestlé generated a return on capital of 13%. The return on capital is the ratio of underlying profits relative to the amount of debt and shareholder capital employed by Nestlé to finance its operations. Nestlé generated a return on equity (profits over shareholder capital) of 16%. These returns are higher than what Nestlé's capital providers (lenders and shareholders) would expect to earn as fair compensation over time, so Nestlé can therefore be said to be generating positive economic value.

For example, in 2013, lenders (bond holders) demanded less than 4% to provide Nestlé with long-term loans. For a typical firm in an economy, an estimate of the cost of equity capital (the fair compensation demanded by shareholders) can be obtained by adding an equity risk premium to the interest rate on long-term government bonds (i.e. the long-term risk-free interest rate). Shareholders may require higher financial compensation for investing in businesses that are more sensitive to the economic cycle and therefore more risky. The equity risk premium is the extra compensation (above the risk-free rate) that shareholders demand for taking on the high risks associated with investing directly in a business. Risk-free rates on long-term government bonds in most of the developed world (where the majority of Nestlé's revenue and profits are derived) were around 2.5% in 2013. Assuming an equity risk premium of 5%, would imply that the cost of equity for Nestlé is 7.5%. This means that over the long run, Nestlé shareholders expect Nestlé's operations to at least earn an average annual return of 7.5% on the equity capital employed in the business. Nestlé's return on equity of 16% in 2013 far exceeds its cost of equity (the hurdle rate for returns on shareholder capital). Shareholders will be more than happy to provide additional capital for Nestlé to expand its business (if it was required)

Creating economic value means that Nestlé generates a profit after paying a fair compensation for all the resources employed to conduct its business, including a fair compensation for capital. Nestlé's profitability is sustainable, and, since the company is generating positive economic value, the firm should be encouraged to employ more financial resources from capital providers to invest and expand its business.

Figure 11.3. Nestlé 2013 Financials

Nestle 2013 financials in millions of US dollars (1 Swiss Franc = 1.08 US$)

Sales of products (A)	101,374
Expenses incurred for the production and sale of products (B)	**86,999**
Cost of goods sold	52,922
Distribution expenses	8,972
Marketing and administration expenses	21,682
Research and development costs	1,653
other expenses	1,770
Profit from operations (C=A-B)	**14,375**
Interest paid on debt (net of interest received on cash) **(D)**	694
profit before tax (E = C-D)	**13,681**
Taxes paid (F)	**3,582**
Nestle's share of profits from Associates and Joint Venture Partners **(G)**	1,390
Profit attributable to Nestle Shareholders (H= E-F+G)	**11,490**
Major uses of cash flows	
Cash flow from operating activities	16,491
Capital expenditure on assets	5,775
Distributions to shareholders mainly in the form of dividends	7,736
Capital Structure	
Total Assets	**132,440**
Property plant and equipment (fixed assets)	29,700
goodwill and other intangible assets from brands and formulations	47,300
inventories and trade receivables (key parts of current assets)	22,660
other assets	32,780
Total Liabilities	**132,440**
Equity	70,400
Debt	23,914
trade payables (key part of current liabilities)	17,600
other liabilities	20,526
Return on Equity (Net profit ÷Equity)	**16%**
Return on Capital (≈ After tax operating profit÷A total debt and equity capital)	**12%**

Source: Nestlé, Author

12

CIVIC VALUES AND ECONOMIC GROWTH

Virtually every commercial transaction has within itself an element of trust. It can plausibly be argued that much of the economic backwardness in the world can be explained by the lack of mutual confidence.
—Kenneth Arrow, a Nobel Prize winner in Economics.

Civic values foster economic and social cooperation, promote economic transactions, and have the potential to support higher living standards. Communities that have invested to build high levels of civic values within ordinary citizens are likely to be governed better, more prosperous, safer, and more harmonious to live in. In such communities, one is likely to observe effective public institutions, low levels of crime and corruption, and healthy relationships between workers and employers and between rich and poor.

Civic values represent an important factor of production; they are a source of intangible capital that can support higher levels of economic growth and superior living standards.

In an environment of strong civic values, the creation of a vibrant and harmonious community ceases to be the sole responsibility of the government, public institutions, or elected officials. Civic consciousness has the power to induce people to invest time and effort to improve social outcomes, especially when there is no economic or personal incentive to do so. Many civic initiatives are not associated with a financial reward or other forms of personal reward such as high levels of prestige. The lack of economic incentives means that a number of initiatives that have the potential to improve social welfare may never be implemented without high levels of civic values.

Civic values have the potential to induce people to invest time and effort to improve social outcomes, especially when there is no economic or personal incentive to do so.

Through strong levels of civic engagement, individuals may be more likely to take personal responsibility for improving the welfare of their own communities. In many communities, civic initiatives from individuals and charitable organizations contribute immeasurably to improving education, public health, and the welfare of the most

162

vulnerable in society. A number of highly reputable education and healthcare institutions were founded and are supported by charitable contributions from members of the community. When a community invests to build and maintain high levels of civic values, it creates the potential for delivering a higher degree of valuable services beyond limitations set by economic incentives. The value of many civic initiatives may not be reflected in a country's gross domestic product or the income levels of households. As such, in countries that have built a considerable amount of civic capital, citizens have the potential to enjoy superior living standards beyond levels that can be justified by the earnings of typical households.

Civic values govern how people relate to each other regardless of their personal incentives or their origins. Taking account of the impact of one's actions on the welfare of others is at the core of building civic values. Once established, individuals carry their civic values with them, wherever they go. The honour code, which is particularly popular in some American schools and universities, is a great example of how to educate young people to take personal responsibility for maintaining a fair and harmonious society. Under the honour code, students individually and voluntarily take an oath not to partake in or encourage acts of academic dishonesty. The idea that the student next to you has pledged not to cheat and has taken personal responsibility to ensure that there is no cheating around him or her (i.e., will proactively report any acts of academic dishonesty), can be very effective in instilling the desirable social norms of honesty and fairness. When a whole community of students have had the opportunity to discuss, understand, and voluntarily uphold the virtue of academic honesty, the public shame that awaits perpetrators of dishonest acts can be highly effective in dissuading people from acting dishonestly.

More generally, educating ordinary members of a community to voluntarily take personal responsibility for integrity, professionalism, and fairness in dealing with others could be potentially more effective than attempts to achieve the same social goals through policing unethical behaviour. When ordinary members of a community make a conscious decision to voluntarily uphold important social norms, they also become more interested in encouraging other members of the community to live by those norms. In other words, the sustainable way of building and maintaining civic values is by democratizing responsibility for upholding these values among ordinary members of a community.

Civic values are necessary to support the proper functioning of any civilized society. Without civic values, laws are weak at protecting and improving social welfare. No law can be detailed enough to precisely deliver all the goals that it was designed to achieve. The ability of the law to protect the welfare of citizens in a community largely depends on their willingness to uphold the law voluntarily. If too many people decide to flout the law at the same time, no law can be enforceable. The most effective law-enforcement office is that of the ordinary citizen. There are a large number of laws and regulations—such as those against theft, smoking in public places, pollution, leaving debris in streets and parks, etc.—that can only deliver their intended social goals through a voluntary commitment by private citizens to abide by these laws and their willingness to police other members of the public to ensure compliance. Because of their invaluable role in delivering the intended social benefits of laws and regulations, governments and law-setting bodies could consult more frequently with ordinary members of the public in the process of setting laws. Public education aimed at explaining the welfare-enhancing goals of laws and regulations should be regarded as a key component of enforcement strategies. More generally, many desirable codes of conduct such as professionalism, integrity, and fairness, which are essential for the proper functioning of any society, may only be delivered in a sustainable manner by fostering personal responsibility among individuals to voluntarily uphold such values even when there is no explicit financial reward for doing so.

Public trust is an essential product of civic capital. Public trust is necessary to promote economic and social interaction within a society. Public trust is a basic level of trust among random members of a community who may not know each other. High levels of public trust enable economic transaction and promote social welfare. An element of trust is a precondition for all economic transactions. For transactions that involve very detailed documentation, for example, an auto-insurance contract or an airline ticket, few people bother to read the fine print because they trust in the decency and professionalism of the providers of these services to honour their promise to deliver. They also trust that service providers will not use details in the fine print to take advantage of their customers. If there was a highly perceived risk that airline tickets might generally not be honoured on the date one planned to travel, the market for air travel would collapse or substantially contract. We trust that the brands of goods we see in supermarkets are the true brands and that weights displayed on products are the true weights. We trust that money will be accepted in exchange for goods and services. We have enough trust to bank and shop online. We trust that our bank balances are real and accurate and that we can access our deposits at our convenience. When we visit health facilities, we trust that the doctors and nurses are primarily devoted to improving our health. Without trust very little economic and social interaction will occur.

An element of trust is a precondition for all economic transactions.

High levels of public trust facilitate transactions because they reduce the cost of obtaining and verifying all the information that may be relevant to making economic decisions. The high cost of obtaining and verifying all aspects of information can limit the number of transactions that can occur when there is not trust. If business transactions required checking and verifying every claim made in documents, many transactions cannot be concluded. A perception that a counterparty may intentionally try to abuse public trust by making false claims, could restrict business transactions to one's family members and close friends and deprive a community of many mutually beneficial opportunities. It is impossible to write contracts or take legal protection against all possible sources of risk. As such, without a basic level of trust, limited transactions will occur.

According to Kenneth Arrow, *"Trust is an important lubricant of a social system. It is extremely efficient; it saves a lot of trouble to have a fair degree of reliance upon other people's word. Unfortunately trust is not an easily purchased commodity: If you have to buy it, you already have some doubts about what you've bought."*

Without public trust, governments will lack confidence to take actions that may be costly in the short-term but that can deliver favourable outcomes in the future. Citizens who do not trust their governments are unlikely to support tough measures when necessary. This contributes to rigidity in government decision-making and can cripple a government's ability to respond to economic and social challenges. Without public trust in the integrity of government spending plans, citizens may lose interest in paying taxes. Without public trust in the ability of the government to manage money supply to deliver price stability, people have few incentives to save, and interest rates are more likely to be high on a structural basis.

Without trust, the ability to mobilize resources from random members of a community for any cause will be compromised. Without public trust in the security of bank deposits, the ability of banks to meet the capital needs of households and firms with investment opportunities will be constrained. Without high levels of public trust in the integrity of financial markets, it may not be possible to separate the ownership of firms from the management. In an environment where the capital resources of firms are limited to the personal wealth of managers, many large corporations that produce invaluable goods to support our quality of life will cease to exist. Without trust, there is limited opportunity for social cooperation and the number of social organizations such as religious bodies, the Red Cross, local charities, and other community initiatives will be severely restricted. Without adequate levels of trust, economic and social interaction is diminished, and living standards may be substantially lower than potential.

Civic values can improve the effectiveness of governments and public institutions. In an environment of strong civic values, elected officials are more dedicated to improving social welfare rather than enriching themselves at the expense of the general public. In such an environment, people are more proactive in paying taxes, and they voluntarily take up responsibility to monitor their governments. When civic values are embedded in the community, one is likely to see a high level of professionalism among public-sector employees and members of the community make judicious use of public resources and social benefits. For example, governments in many countries provide unemployment benefits primarily to reduce human suffering in times of joblessness. Every worker pays taxes and may be entitled to receive financial support during periods of unemployment. However, civic consciousness will dictate that people who are fortunate enough to have strong personal finances should opt out of receiving state aid in times of joblessness. This is because, the spirit of the unemployment benefit (i.e., to support people in times of financial need) is far more important than the legal provision that entitles everyone to receive such payments (when they are unemployed).

The penalty for poor civic values and low levels of public trust is most clearly seen in the way communities deal with natural disaster or accidents such as fires, epidemics, hurricanes, and earthquakes. In these extremely challenging circumstances, low levels of public trust can compound human agony and loss. Natural disaster sparks fear in people and sharpens an individual's instinct for self-preservation. However, uncoordinated self-preservation efforts in these circumstances may endanger more lives. For example, when there is a major risk of a highly contagious disease spreading, low levels of public trust reduce the willingness of citizens to follow the directions and advice of health officials and may put a greater number of people at risk. When there is some major accident that threatens people's lives in a densely populated location, for example, a fire outbreak in a major train station, stadium, or theater, if everyone were to follow their natural self-preservation instincts and rush for the exit, many more lives would be lost. In this situation, many of the deaths would be the direct result of the stampede that would likely ensue in the rush for the exit(s). In periods of disaster, high levels of public trust in the ability of public officials to coordinate an effective response can help subdue potentially disruptive self-preservation actions and support a much better outcome.

Data from the World Values Survey shows a strong correlation between living standards and the level of public trust in countries. In response to the question: "Generally speaking, would you say that most people can be trusted or that you need to be very careful in dealing with people?", residents of Norway, Finland, and Denmark were the most trustful; two out of three people agreed that most people can be trusted. Between 30 and 50 percent of people in northern European countries, the United Kingdom, the United States, and both emerging and high-income nations in Asia (Japan, China, and Korea) agree that most people can be trusted. Levels of public trust in southern Europe is low, around 20 percent. Levels of public trust in Latin America are even lower, between 10 and 20 percent. Countries with the lowest levels of public trust are concentrated in Africa and the Mediterranean. In countries like Ghana, Rwanda, and Turkey, less than 10 percent of people agree that most people can be trusted. Conditions that foster or destroy public trust differ across nations. For example, countries like Rwanda that are recovering from civil war and genocide are less likely to have high levels of public trust when compared to countries that have sustained long periods of political stability. A country's history on governance, political stability, civil rights, rights of the poor, fight against corruption, access to a fair trial and justice, religious freedom, and social harmony may have an impact on the willingness of citizens to trust random people and key institutions. Countries that have invested to build and maintain high levels of integrity and fairness in effective public institutions often have high levels of public trust.

The level of civic values in a community can be indirectly assessed by the weight of public anger associated with generally undesirable behaviour such as cheating in school, corruption, and legal injustice (i.e., where there is no fair trial). When desirable social norms are not embedded within ordinary members of the community, the legal and social penalties associated with abusing public trust is low; as such, people may be more likely to promote their individual ambitions at the expense of the community. When actions that abuse public trust go unpunished, they can lose their stigma, and social evils such as corruption can become "acceptable" as part of the normal course of doing business. In an environment of general apathy towards upholding civic values, a community becomes more vulnerable to abuses, and social welfare and living standards cannot be maximized. In order to promote social welfare, it is important to uphold a values system where ordinary people are inspired to uphold certain basic social norms without exceptions. For example, integrity and fairness form two important foundations of public trust. There should be broad social acceptance that comes from exhibiting these values and an absolute shaming of people who cheat or break the law irrespective of their levels of wealth or influence.

The degree to which civic values are embedded in a community tends to be self-reinforcing. This means that it may be extremely challenging to break a culture of poor civic values and build good ones. However, irrespective of the starting point, efforts to build civic values, if sustained, could generate highly rewarding benefits in the long term. When ordinary members of a community successfully cooperate to address one challenge, they become more open to cooperating in the future.

Ordinary people and communities will only bother to invest in civic values when they have been educated to understand the invaluable role civic values play in promoting individual and social welfare. Building civic values is a long-term investment that has the potential to deliver invaluable rewards. The process of building civil values may be challenging and takes time. However, because it involves cultural norms that bind people together, once decent levels of civic values take root in a society, they are more likely to be maintained.

Societies that find the resources in political leadership, religion, education, and other institutions to promote civic values and general trust are likely to derive long-term benefits from this investment. Building civic values involves inspiring people to reflect on the consequences of certain actions on the welfare of the general public. In the absence of any legal penalties or meaningful public shame, acts such as cheating and corruption can carry strong personal rewards but may ultimately ruin the welfare of the general public by restricting economic and social interaction. When ordinary people have had an opportunity to internalize the large social and economic cost associated with individual acts of dishonesty, they may be more likely to uphold an uncompromising position against such vices.

Since civic values play a crucial role in improving living standards, perhaps they could be given more attention in education curricula and broader public-education initiatives. Schools present an excellent platform to inspire civic consciousness. Students should be inspired to think about the consequences of their actions on others and learn to appreciate the importance of upholding integrity even when no one is looking. Young people should be encouraged to take personal initiative to act honourably rather than be forced to follow rules blindly or strong-armed into obeying rules without given an opportunity to understand and personally accept why certain actions may be undesirable for themselves and the community in the long-term. Students should be treated as responsible citizens in the making whose values will determine the nature of society in the future.

Like all other forms of capital, civic capital is costly to provide (in the time and effort required to inculcate civic values) but it has the potential to deliver attractive long-term rewards. Communities in which ordinary citizens have been educated to appreciate the potentially attractive return associated with an investment in civic values are more likely to allocate resources to build this invaluable capital.

Within every community, there are numerous opportunities for ordinary people to plant seeds of civic capital. People who have benefited from voluntary civic initiatives and educated to understand the motivations of the volunteers are more likely to demonstrate civic initiatives later in life. This means that individuals or small groups can initiate a micro civic-capital investment that is likely to be sustainable in its own small way. People can be inspired to proactively volunteer their services in the delivery of desirable social goals. For example, if parents and community members take greater interest in schools and occasionally volunteer to discuss their career and industry experiences, share hobbies or professional skills, and help with particular school programs, schools can be empowered to provide a better education. Many people in the community go through periods when they are less engaged and could devote a small portion of their time to activities that promote social welfare. Students may have a lot of time on their hands during holidays. Retired people may have more time on their hands than young parents, and people who are temporarily out of work, may be able to spare some time to engage with their communities.

Communities and institutions that want to foster a culture of volunteering need to be more proactive in creating programs that encourage people to efficiently sign up and engage in meaningful activities. Institutions can be more proactive in marketing volunteering opportunities through schools, businesses and social networking platforms. When volunteering becomes frustrating because of bureaucracy or when institutions do not openly welcome and encourage such activities, public interest in volunteering is less likely to flourish. People who invest in civic initiatives are likely to feel better about themselves for creating value within the community. If one has the time to spare, helping to teach poor children in the community to read or volunteering in local hospitals out of genuine interest are likely to be rewarding activities. Economic engagement is not the only way for individuals to create value for their communities (and themselves), and the opportunity to create value for society does not end when people retire from active employment.

Since civic values are instrumental in supporting economic growth and living standards over the long term, targets for maintaining and improving civic values could be part of the economic and social policies of elected governments. It might be useful for elected governments to assess the level of trust that citizens have in government and public institutions. Ideally, surveys showing the level of public trust in the government, trust in judicial fairness, perceptions of corruption and confidence in the effectiveness of key public institutions could be monitored over time to see how a society is progressing on building or eroding civic capital.

The liberty to engage in initiatives that promote one's welfare is a fundamental pillar of economic progress. However, low levels of civic values within a community place limits on the ability of individuals to improve their well-being. A key component of maximizing an individual's well-being is inherently linked to the ability of random members of a community to cooperate in economic and social initiatives. Without the voluntary cooperation of ordinary citizens, the ability of governments to adequately deliver public services may be compromised. Without adequate levels of public trust, it may not be possible to mobilize resources from random members of the general public, and the production of many welfare-enhancing goods and services may be restricted. Building adequate levels of civic capital should therefore be an integral component of individuals' initiatives to enhance their welfare.

ABOUT THE AUTHOR

Franklin Adatsi is a graduate of Brown University and Oxford University. He has over ten years of experience in the finance industry. His career experience spans financial markets in the United States, Europe, and global emerging markets. Franklin believes that a greater understanding of economic issues in an increasingly interdependent world can support stronger governance standards and economic progress. All proceeds from the sale of this book will be dedicated to economics and civic education initiatives.

www.ingramcontent.com/pod-product-compliance
Lightning Source LLC
Chambersburg PA
CBHW082304200526

45168CB00018B/3223